Cooking with Spice

Culinary Secrets
from Turkey to Morocco

Edited by Fred Sandman

BARNES & NOBLE

NEW YORK

contents

Culinary Temptations
From Turkey to Morocco

It's not really surprising that the cuisine of this area is as varied as it is, considering the geographic reach of this area. Thus the "land of the rising sun" stretches from Turkey to Iran and the Arabian peninsula right across North Africa to Morocco. It is the specialty of each individual country, together with the respective cultural customs, that make the cuisine of this region so varied. And as multifarious as the individual dishes may be, the dishes themselves are extravagant and extensive. But only in the evenings, as breakfast and the midday meal are only small snacks because of the heat. It is not until it gets cooler in the evenings that the main meal is served. And whoever has had the good fortune of enjoying the hospitality of these countries will be impressed by the selection of wonderful appetizers (called *mezze*), the incredible vegetable dishes, the elaborate meat and fish dishes as well as the exquisitely sweet, heavy desserts that are served. Here people consider it their duty to bestow their hospitality on everyone, no matter whether friend or stranger, and not spare any cost in the process.

1

MINT (left) has a refreshing aroma and a spicy, peppery flavor. It goes well with sweet foods and also with salty ones. Freshly brewed mint tea is also very popular from Morocco to Jordan.

1 COUSCOUS is a staple foodstuff here. This semolina comes from hard wheat or millet. It is served with meat, fish and vegetables, but also as a sweet main meal. Instant couscous is especially practical because it is quick to prepare.

2 SAFFRON is the most expensive spice in the world. You can buy it powdered or as threads, and only ever use tiny quantities at a time.

2

3

3 **CUCUMBERS**, like other vegetables, play a big role in Oriental appetizers and main dishes.

4 **YUFKA PASTRY** is much like puff pastry, forming many layers when baked. It is perfect for pastry packets, pasties and sweet desserts.

5 **HONEY** is a must in Mediterranean cuisine; it is used to sweeten desserts and baking, but also for the seasoning of dips and ragouts. Fruit preserves such as quince or apricots may be used instead.

6 **DRIED FRUITS** such as dates, apricots and raisins are firm favorites not just for preparing desserts, but also for flavoring many salty dishes.

7 **ROSEWATER** is rose oil made from rose petals and dissolved in water. It gives puddings and pastries an exquisite flavor. It is available from pharmacies or large food stores.

7

HARISSA is an extremely hot North African chili pepper paste flavored with garlic and spices. It is available ready-made in tubes or cans. You can also make your own version of harissa quite easily (see page 9).

LEGUMES such as chickpeas, beans and lentils are favorite ingredients for vegetarian dishes and braised dishes. They are often used in exciting combinations with other ingredients and flavored with garlic, onions, spices and herbs. Hummus (or humus), a dip made from chickpeas, is frequently served as an appetizer.

YOGURT is still made at home in many households from Turkey to Morocco. It is tarter than our yogurt and contains more fat. Therefore you should only use full-fat yogurt when preparing one of these dishes.

RAS EL HANOUT is an aromatic, hot blend of spices that is used in Algeria, Morocco and Tunisia to flavor meat, fish and vegetable dishes.

SHEEP and **GOAT CHEESES** are eaten in many Mediterranean countries. Both types are also popular as fillings.

SESAME PASTE or Tahini (also known as Tahin or Tehina) is a paste consisting of ground sesame seeds. It is mainly used in dips, but also flavors other dishes. Stir well before using, as the oils tend to separate at the top.

6

POMEGRANATES have been cultivated around the Mediterranean for ages. Their juice refines the dish with a fine, tart flavor, while the seeds are used for desserts and salads.

5

Step by Step
Delicacies from Arabian Nights

Bread is the staple food from Turkey to Morocco, besides couscous, bulgar, millet and rice. There is hardly a meal that is not served with bread – mainly pita bread using yeast. Pita bread is still baked at home in many families, and garnished with a variety of spices or seeds. Apropros spices, they are an absolute must in the Mediterranean kitchen, and there's not one bazaar that does not offer a wide variety of spices, herbs, special flavorings and distilled essences such as rosewater. Apart from that, pickled salted lemons and a variety of spice mixtures and pastes (e.g. harissa) are used to give mezze, vegetables, meat and fish dishes their distinct flavors. Puddings or pastries are usually reserved for guests and celebrations. People do not eat them as dessert at mealtime. The most popular drinks, apart from water, are black tea and mint tea, coffee and ayran (yogurt with water); almond milk is also appreciated as a refresher (see page 126). The Koran prohibits the consumption of alcohol.

Baking pita bread

1 Heat ½ cup milk in a pan. Crumble 1 ounce fresh yeast into the lukewarm milk and stir.

2 In a large mixing bowl mix 5 cups all-purpose flour with 2 teaspoons salt. Add the yeast milk and, gradually, ¾ cup water to the flour.

3 Knead all together to make a smooth, elastic dough. Cover and leave for 40 minutes in a warm place to rise.

4 Knead the dough thoroughly again, cut in half, and make into two round, flat patties with a thicker edge.

5 Mix 1 egg yolk with 1 tablespoon olive oil and 2 teaspoons sugar thoroughly in a small bowl.

6 Brush the dough patties with the egg-oil mixture. Sprinkle with white sesame seeds. Bake for about 15 minutes at 450°F.

Preparing salted lemons

1 Wash 10 lemons in hot water and rub dry. Cut into the lemons cross-wise 1/3-inch deep, but do not cut right through.

2 Fill each lemon with a little salt, and press together firmly.

3 Fill a little salt into a large, tall canning jar. Layer the lemons inside, repeatedly sprinkling with salt.

4 Squeeze out 2 lemons, and pour the juice over the salted lemons. Fill with boiling water and leave to marinate for about 4 weeks.

Brewing mint tea

1 Pour 1/2 cup boiling water over 2 tablespoons green tea in a pot. Then empty the water out again.

2 Brew the tea with 2 cups boiling water and stir in 4 tablespoons sugar. Add 1 bunch fresh mint and allow the tea to steep for 2-3 minutes.

Preparing harissa

1 Cut 1 3/4 ounces dried red chili peppers in half lengthwise and remove the seeds. Cover with boiling water and allow to stand for 20 minutes.

2 Peel 2 garlic cloves and chop coarsely. Crush with a mortar and pestle adding a little salt.

3 Grind together the chilies, garlic, 1 tea-spoon caraway seeds, 1 1/2 teaspoons ground cumin and 2 teaspoons coriander seeds.

4 Stir 1-2 tablespoons olive oil into the paste and fill into a screw-top jar. Cover harissa with olive oil and keep in the fridge.

Mezze
and Soups

Stuffed Grape Leaves
with Rice and Raisins

Well-wrapped the battle is half won: Your guests will love
these small delicacies with their juicy fillings

Ingredients

2 small onions

1 tablespoon sesame oil

1/3 cup long-grain rice

2 tablespoons pine nuts

4 sprigs cilantro

2 tablespoons raisins

1/2 teaspoon ground cinnamon

about 20 grape leaves

(pickled in brine)

juice of 1 lemon

lemon slices, to garnish

Preparation

MAKES ABOUT 10

1 For the filling, peel the onions and dice finely. Heat the oil in a pan and cook the onions until translucent. Add the rice and also cook until translucent. Add 1/2 cup water, cover the rice and cook for 30 minutes over very low heat.

2 Roast the pine nuts in a pan without oil until golden. Wash the cilantro and shake dry, pluck the leaves from the stems and chop finely. Add with the pine nuts, the raisins and cinnamon to the rice.

3 Rinse the grape leaves under running cold water, dab dry and remove the stems. Take 2 leaves (or one if using large leaves), put 1 heaped tablespoon filling onto the lower end of the grape leaves, fold the sides in, then roll up the leaves.

4 Distribute the stuffed leaves evenly in a wide pan, sprinkle with lemon juice and cover with water. Cover and simmer for about 30 minutes over low heat. Remove the lid, then simmer the rolls for another 10-15 minutes until almost all the liquid has evaporated.

5 Allow the stuffed grape leaves to cool and serve in a dish with the lemon slices. Pita bread goes well with the stuffed leaves.

Spicy Falafel
with Yogurt Dip

The favorite snack from Turkey to Morocco: These nutty seasoned chickpea croquettes are sold at every street corner in the Middle East

Ingredients

2 cups dried chickpeas

1 onion · 1 garlic clove

1 sprig each parsley and cilantro

1-2 tablespoons olive oil

2-3 tablespoons breadcrumbs

ground cumin and coriander

salt · freshly ground pepper

vegetable oil, for frying

1 cup plain yogurt

3 tablespoons sesame paste (Tahini; ready-made)

1 tablespoon honey

1/2 teaspoon grated rind of an orange

1/2 teaspoon each ground allspice and cinnamon

Preparation

SERVES 4

1   Soak the chickpeas in cold water overnight. Pour into a sieve the next day, rinse with cold water and allow to drain.

2   Peel the onion and garlic and dice finely. Add both to the chickpeas and process in a blender. Wash both the parsley and cilantro and dab dry, pluck the leaves from the stems and chop finely.

3   Mix the chickpea mixture with the herbs, oil and breadcrumbs. Season well with cumin, coriander, salt and pepper. Wet your hands, and shape into finger-sized croquettes.

4   Heat the oil in a pan or deep-fryer to 350°F, and fry the falafel in batches, without crowding them, until crisp and golden brown, turning them over once. Remove with a ladle, allow to drain on kitchen paper and keep in a warm place.

5   For the dip, mix the yogurt well with the sesame paste, honey, orange rind and spices. Season with salt and pepper to taste. Serve the yogurt dip with the falafel.

Tip

If you need to make this quickly, use 2 small tins of chickpeas (at about 9 ounces drained weight each), then you won't need to soak the chickpeas for several hours, or overnight.

Potato Croquettes
with Bulgur and Herbs

*Spuds in a different light: These spicy balls with herbs and
ground wheat are a welcome and delicious alternative to chips*

Ingredients

14 ounces waxy potatoes

salt · 1 1/3 cups bulgur

2 cups vegetable stock

1 onion · 2 garlic cloves

1 cup ricotta · 1 egg

1-2 tablespoons all-purpose
flour

2 tablespoons each chopped
parsley and oregano

freshly ground pepper

ground paprika (sweet)

vegetable oil, for frying

Preparation

SERVES 4

1 Peel the potatoes, wash and cook for about 15 minutes in salt
water. Pour off, allow to drain and grate while still warm.

2 Cook the bulgur with the stock in a pan, remove from the
heat, cover and allow to swell for 15 minutes.

3 Peel and dice the onion and garlic finely. Mix the still warm
grated potato with the bulgur, diced onion and garlic, cream
cheese, egg, flour and herbs. Season well with salt, pepper
and paprika and allow to cool. Wet your hands and form the
potato mixture into small balls.

4 Heat the oil in a pan or deep fryer to about 350°F and fry the
potato croquettes until golden brown. Remove, allow to drain
on paper towels, then serve warm or cold.

Tip

The potato croquettes are a rustic complement
to a tomato salad or the tomato preserves on
page 23. Hummus (see the recipe on page 28) also
makes a nice dip to serve with the croquettes.

Orange Salad
with Olives and Fennel

Ingredients

1 fennel bulb

1/2 lemon

salt

freshly ground pepper

4 tablespoons olive oil

3 oranges

1 pomegranate

5 ounces black olives (pitted)

1/2 bunch mint

Preparation

SERVES 4

1 Wash and prepare the fennel, separate the
   leaves. Cut the leaves in fine slices. For the
   marinade, squeeze the lemon and season the
   juice with salt, pepper and oil.

2 Peel one of the oranges with a sharp knife,
   removing the white pith. Lift out the fruit
   segments from the membrane, catching any
   juice. Squeeze the other 2 oranges and add all
   the juices to the marinade.

3 Mix the fennel slices and the orange segments
   in a mixing bowl together with the marinade
   and leave in the fridge for about 20 minutes.

4 Cut the pomegranate in half and scoop out the
   seeds with a teaspoon. Discard the pith and
   mix the shiny pink seeds into the salad with
   the olives. Wash the mint and shake dry. Pluck
   the leaves from the stems, chop two thirds of
   the leaves coarsely and fold into the salad.
   Serve the orange salad in small bowls and garnish with the remaining mint leaves.

Carrot Salad
with Orange Vinaigrette

Ingredients

1 pound carrots

5 oranges

1 lemon

3 tablespoons orange-
blossom water

3 tablespoons sugar

salt

freshly ground white pepper

ground cinnamon, for dusting

cumin seeds, to garnish

Preparation

SERVES 4

1 Wash the carrots, peel and grate. Peel two oranges, removing the pith. Lift out the fruit segments from their membranes and dice finely. Mix with the grated carrot.

2 Squeeze the other 3 oranges and the lemon. To prepare a vinaigrette, mix the citrus juices together with the orange-blossom water, sugar and ¼ teaspoon each salt and pepper.

3 Pour the vinaigrette over the grated carrot and diced orange. Cover the salad with plastic wrap and leave for about 1 hour in the fridge to marinate.

4 To serve, arrange carrot salad on plates or in small bowls, dust with cinnamon and sprinkle with cumin.

Tabbouleh
with Parsley

A medley of green, white and red: These colors guarantee
culinary highlights not just in Lebanon

Ingredients

1/2 cup couscous (or bulgur)

salt

3 medium ripe tomatoes

6 cups chopped parsley

4 scallions

1/2 bunch mint

juice of 2 lemons

8 tablespoons olive oil

freshly ground pepper

Preparation

SERVES 4

1 Fill the couscous into a bowl and salt. Add lukewarm water –
it should cover the grains by the width of your finger.
Allow the couscous to swell for about 45 minutes (1 hour
for bulgur).

2 Cut an X into the top and bottom of the tomatoes. Put into
boiling hot water for about 30 seconds. The skin should come
off now. Peel, quarter and seed. Dice the quartered tomatoes
finely. Wash the parsley and shake dry, pluck the leaves from
the stems and chop coarsely. Wash and trim the scallions, cut
into fine rings.

3 Pour the couscous into a sieve and allow to drain. Mix with
the vegetables and parsley in a bowl. Wash the mint and
shake dry, pluck the leaves from the stems and chop finely.
Stir with lemon juice, oil, salt and pepper to make a vinaigrette, then mix with the couscous salad.

Tip

This salad is also ideal as a light summer meal.
Make it more substantial by adding golden brown
fried strips of chicken or turkey breast.

Bean Salad
with Herbs and Onions

Ingredients

1 ³/₄ cups dried fava beans

(or black beans)

3 garlic cloves

1 tomato

1 bunch parsley

juice of 2 lemons

¹/₂ cup olive oil

salt · freshly ground pepper

¹/₂ teaspoon ground cumin

Preparation

SERVES 4

1 Wash the beans and allow to swell overnight in ample cold water. Bring to a boil the next day in the same water, cover and cook over low heat for about 1 hour until done.

2 Meanwhile peel the garlic and dice finely. Cut an X into the top and bottom of the tomato. Put into boiling hot water for about 30 seconds. The skin should come off now. Peel, quarter and seed. Dice the quartered tomato finely.

3 Wash the parsley and shake dry, pluck the leaves from the stems and chop finely. Mix with the lemon juice, oil, garlic and diced tomato. Season the marinade with salt, pepper and cumin.

4 Pour the beans into a sieve, allow to drain and mix with the marinade. Cover and allow to marinate overnight in the fridge.

Tomato Preserves
with White Sesame

Ingredients

6 large ripe tomatoes

$\frac{1}{2}$ cup olive oil

4 tablespoons white
sesame seeds

1-2 tablespoons honey

salt

freshly ground white pepper

Preparation

SERVES 4

1 Preheat the oven to 275°F. Wash the tomatoes, arrange in an ovenproof dish and pour the oil over. Bake for about 20 minutes on the middle rack of the oven until done.

2 Meanwhile roast the sesame seeds without oil in a pan over low heat until they turn golden. Set aside on a plate.

3 Remove the tomatoes from the oven and allow to cool. Peel, quarter and seed. Dice the quartered tomatoes finely.

4 Heat the honey in a pan. Add the diced tomatoes, season with salt and pepper and simmer for about 2 minutes over low heat.

5 Fill the tomato preserves into a bowl, sprinkle with sesame seeds and allow to cool. Serve with pita bread (optional).

Puff Pastry Turnovers
with Ground Meat Filling

A tasty filling in a crunchy casing: Each bite of these small
Turkish moons with their spicy meat filling is a sheer delight

Ingredients

1 pound puff pastry (frozen,
10 square sheets)

½ bunch scallions

1 garlic clove

1 tablespoon olive oil

1 pound ground beef

1 teaspoon each ground cumin
and coriander

½ teaspoon ground cinnamon

salt · freshly ground pepper

8 cherry tomatoes

2 tablespoons chopped parsley

1 egg yolk · 2 tablespoons milk

Preparation

MAKES 10

1 Arrange the sheets of pastry alongside one another on a dishtowel and allow to defrost. Wash and prepare the scallions, cut into fine rings. Peel the garlic and dice finely.

2 Heat the oil in a pan, add the beef and fry until crumbly. Add the scallions, garlic and spices, and fry all together for about 3 minutes. Allow the mixture to cool.

3 Preheat the oven to 400°F. Line a baking sheet with baking parchment. Cut 10 circles (about 4 inches across) out of the sheets of pastry. Wash the tomatoes, halve and dice finely. Mix into the beef mixture with the parsley. Arrange the mixture on the pastry circles, fold the pastry together over the top, press together firmly at the edges and shape into moons.

4 Arrange the moons on the baking tray. Mix the egg yolk with the milk and brush over the moons. Bake for about 25 minutes on the middle rack of the oven until golden.

Tip

For variation, fill the pastry with chicken. Wash 2 skinless, boneless chicken breast portions, dab dry, dice finely and sear. Then continue as given above.

Millet Bakes
with Bell Peppers and Olives

Healthy food can be so good: There's no need for a
guilty conscience if you take a second helping

Ingredients

1 ⅓ cup millet

2 tablespoons olive oil

2 ½ cups vegetable stock

1 red bell pepper

1 garlic clove

2 ounces black olives

(pitted) · 3 eggs

½ cup low-fat ricotta

(or soft cheese)

2 teaspoons each chopped

rosemary and sage · salt

freshly ground pepper

ground paprika (sweet)

clarified butter, for frying

Preparation

SERVES 4

1 Rinse the millet in a sieve under running cold water and allow to drain well. Heat the oil in the pan and fry the millet until golden. Add the stock, cover the pan and allow the millet to swell for about 40 minutes over low heat. Remove the pan from the heat and allow to cool.

2 Cut the pepper in half lengthwise, seed, wash and dice finely. Peel the garlic and dice finely. Chop the olives finely.

3 Separate two eggs. Mix the egg yolks with the remaining egg, the ricotta, olives, diced pepper and herbs into the millet. Season the millet mixture with salt, pepper and paprika. Whisk the egg whites until stiff and fold them into the mixture.

4 Wet your hands and shape the millet mixture into palm-sized round pasties. Heat the butter in portions in a non-stick skillet, and fry the flats on either side until golden. Remove from the skillet, allow to drain on paper towels, and serve hot or cold.

Tip

If you like your millet bakes spicy-hot, mix 1 finely diced red chili pepper into the millet mixture. Serve the millet patties with yogurt dip (see page 14) or sesame dip (see page 30).

Hummus
with Cumin

Ingredients

1 ¾ cups dried chickpeas

3 garlic cloves

salt

2 lemons

½ cup sesame paste (Tahini, ready-made)

¼ teaspoon ground cumin

a few sprigs of parsley

4 tablespoons olive oil

16 black olives (pitted)

lemon wedges, to garnish

Preparation

SERVES 4

1 Allow the chickpeas to soak in cold water overnight. Drain in a sieve the next day, rinse with cold water, allow to drain, fill into a pan, cover with water, and allow to simmer for about 40 minutes over low heat.

2 Pour the chickpeas into a sieve, rinse under cold running water and allow to drain. Blend in a bowl with an immersion blender or in a food processor. Peel the garlic and crush with a little salt using a mortar and pestle, then blend into the chickpea paste.

3 Squeeze the lemons. Mix the lemon juice, sesame paste and cumin into the chickpea paste. Season the hummus to taste with salt, cover and leave for about 30 minutes in the fridge to marinate.

4 Wash the parsley, shake dry and chop the stems coarsely. Arrange the hummus in small bowls, and press a well in the center with a teaspoon. Drizzle the oil into the well, garnish the chickpea paste with the olives, parsley and lemon wedges. Serve with pita bread (optional).

Baba Ghanoush
with Parsley and Harissa

Ingredients

2 large eggplants (1 pound)

3 tablespoons olive oil

1 garlic clove

½ bunch parsley

juice of 1 lemon

2 tablespoons sesame paste
(Tahini, ready-made)

about ½ teaspoon harissa
(see page 9)

salt

freshly ground pepper

Preparation

SERVES 4

1 Preheat the oven to 425°F. Line a baking sheet with baking parchment. Wash the eggplants, rub dry, prick several times with a fork and brush with 1 tablespoon oil. Place on the middle rack of the oven and bake for about 45-60 minutes until soft inside.

2 Peel the garlic and chop coarsely. Wash the parsley and shake dry, pluck the leaves from the stems and chop coarsely. Squeeze out the lemon.

3 Remove the eggplants from the oven, cover with a damp dishtowel and allow to cool for a moment. Peel off the skin, scraping the pulp from the back of the skin if necessary. Chop the cooled pulp coarsely.

4 Blend the eggplants together with the sesame paste, garlic, parsley, lemon juice and the remaining oil in a food processor. Season to taste with harissa, salt and pepper. Serve with pita bread.

Sesame Dip
with Cream Yogurt

Easy, but indescribably delicious: This rich dip is a perfect match for pita bread, vegetable sticks and falafel

Ingredients

4 1/2 ounces sesame paste
(Tahini, ready-made)

3 garlic cloves

1/4 cup lemon juice

3 tablespoons plain whole-
milk yogurt

1/2 teaspoon each ground
coriander and cumin

salt · 2 tablespoons white
sesame seeds

Preparation

SERVES 4

1 Stir the sesame paste well until smooth, measure out the required amount and fill into a small bowl. Peel the garlic, dice finely and stir into the sesame mixture.

2 Stir the lemon juice into the sesame-garlic mixture, gradually adding about 1/4 cup cold water.

3 Fold in the yogurt. Season the dip to taste with coriander, cumin and salt, cover and leave to marinate in the fridge for about 2 hours.

4 To serve, roast the sesame seeds in a skillet without any oil over medium heat until golden brown. Sprinkle over the sesame dip. Serve with warm pita bread or falafel (see page 14).

Tip

Sesame is very popular in the oriental cuisine. The seeds have a mild nutty flavor that becomes stronger when roasted. Sesame is available white, brown and black.

Chickpea Balls
with Chili Dip

*This appetizer could become a habit: These small balls
are the promising prelude to an exciting dish*

Ingredients

For the balls:

1 ¼ cups chickpeas (canned)

1 lemon · 1 cup breadcrumbs

1 teaspoon chili powder

½ teaspoon ground cumin

salt · 1 egg

vegetable oil, for frying

For the dip:

3 tablespoons mayonnaise

2 tablespoons chili sauce

1 tablespoon tomato ketchup

Preparation

SERVES 4

1 For the balls, pour the chickpeas into a sieve and allow to drain well. Wash the lemon with hot water and rub dry. Grate the rind finely and squeeze the lemon.

2 Fill the chickpeas into a high-rimmed mixing bowl with the lemon rind, lemon juice, bread crumbs, chili, cumin and 1 teaspoon salt and blend with a hand mixer until fine. Mix the egg into the mixture.

3 With your wet hands, shape the chickpea mix into 12 balls. Heat the oil in the deep fryer or pan and gradually deep-fry the balls until golden brown. Remove from the oil and allow to drain on paper towels.

4 For the dip, stir the mayonnaise together with the chili sauce and ketchup in a small bowl. Place the chickpea balls onto small wooden skewers and serve with the chili dip.

Tip

If preferred, add finely chopped fresh herbs (e.g. a mixture of parsley and cilantro, or parsley and mint) to the chickpea mixture.

Lentil Soup
with Green Bell Pepper

Ingredients

1 ½ cups red lentils

1 small onion

2 garlic cloves

1 green bell pepper

2 tablespoons olive oil

2 ½ cups vegetable stock

salt · freshly ground pepper

1 teaspoon ground cumin

juice of ½ lemon

chervil leaves, to garnish

Preparation
SERVES 4

1 Wash the lentils in a sieve under cold running water and allow to drain. Peel the onion and garlic and chop finely. Cut the pepper in half lengthwise, seed, wash and cut into thin strips.

2 Heat the oil in a pan. Fry the diced onion and garlic until translucent. Add the lentils and the stock.

3 Bring everything to a boil, then simmer for 10 minutes, stirring occasionally. Add the bell pepper, allow soup to cook for about 15 minutes until the lentils are done, but not overcooked.

4 Season soup to taste with salt, pepper, cumin and lemon juice. Arrange in soup bowls or small dishes and garnish with chervil leaves. Serve with pita bread (optional).

Lamb Soup
with Dates and Limes

Ingredients

1 ¼ pounds of lamb shank
(deboned)

2 small onions

2 garlic cloves

2 tablespoons olive oil

2 bay leaves

salt

freshly ground pepper

10 ounces fresh dates

juice of 3 limes

a little ground aniseed and
cloves

parsley leaves, to garnish

Preparation
SERVES 4

1 Remove the fat and sinews from the lamb shanks, and cut the meat into 1-inch cubes. Peel the onions and garlic and dice finely.

2 Heat the oil in a pan in portions and brown the diced meat on all sides. Return all the meat to the pan, add the onions and garlic and fry for another 3 minutes.

3 Add 6 cups water and the bay leaves. Season the soup with salt and pepper, cover and allow to simmer for about 30 minutes.

4 Peel the dates, cut in half and remove the pit. Add to the soup together with the lime juice and heat quickly. Season the lamb soup to taste with aniseed, ground cloves and salt. Serve in soup plates or dishes. Garnish with parsley leaves and serve with pita bread.

Lamb Soup
with Bulgur and Mint

*Three cheers for traditions: This old Algerian soup recipe
captures the region's culture and resources beautifully*

Ingredients

10 ounces lamb (shoulder)

1 onion

1 large bunch cilantro

4 tablespoons olive oil

salt · freshly ground pepper

1 teaspoon ground paprika
(hot)

1 teaspoon dried mint

1 cup bulgur

1 tablespoon tomato paste

Preparation

SERVES 4

1 Cut the lamb into very thin strips. Peel the onions and dice finely. Wash the cilantro and shake dry, pluck the leaves from the stems and chop finely.

2 Heat the oil in a pan, glaze the diced onion and meat in the oil. Add 6 cups water and half the cilantro. Season to taste with salt, pepper, paprika and mint. Add the bulgur. Stir the tomato paste with 2 tablespoons water until smooth, and add to the mixture. Cover and gently cook over low heat for about 45 minutes.

3 Stir in the remaining cilantro and season the soup to taste once more with salt and pepper. Arrange in soup bowls or dishes and serve with lemon slices and pita bread (optional).

Tip

Bulgur consists of whole wheat kernels that have been boiled, then dried and ground. Its nutty flavor makes bulgur an ideal accompaniment to soup, as well as to meat, fish and vegetables.

Arabian Vegetable Soup
with Chicken Breast

Ingredients

1 pound mixed green leaf vegetables (e.g. spinach, Swiss chard)

salt

4 cups chicken stock

about 1 pound chicken breast

1 onion

2 garlic cloves

1 carrot

2 celery sticks

1 tablespoon clarified butter

freshly ground pepper

2-3 tablespoons lemon juice

1 teaspoon grated rind of an orange

Preparation

SERVES 4

1 Prepare and wash the leafy vegetables and cook in boiling salted water for 1-2 minutes. Pour into a sieve, rinse with cold water and allow to drain. Bring the stock to a boil. Wash the chicken breasts, dab dry and allow to simmer in the stock for about 10 minutes.

2 Peel the onion and garlic and dice finely. Wash and peel the carrots. Wash the celery. Cut both into thin strips. Lift the chicken out of the stock, set aside, and pour the stock through a fine sieve.

3 Heat the clarified butter in a large pan. Sauté the onion, garlic and strips of vegetable over medium heat. Add the stock and heat, but do not allow to boil. Simmer the soup gently for about 20 minutes until done.

4 Cut the chicken into thin strips. Add to the soup, along with the leafy vegetables, and heat briefly. Season the soup with salt, pepper, lemon juice and rind, then serve in soup bowls or small dishes.

Cold Cucumber Soup
with Cumin

Ingredients

2 medium cucumbers

2 ¾ cups plain whole-milk yogurt

about ¾ cup carbonated
mineral water

3 garlic cloves

1-2 teaspoons cumin seeds

½ teaspoon coarse salt

salt · freshly ground pepper

Preparation

SERVES 4

1 Peel the cucumbers and cut in half lengthwise.
Seed with a teaspoon. Dice the cucumber
halves finely and blend in a food processor.

2 Stir the yogurt and the mineral water together
well in a bowl. Peel the garlic cloves and
squeeze through a garlic press. Fold the
cucumber paste into the garlic yogurt.

3 Roast the cumin in a pan without any oil, until
aromatic. Crush lightly with a mortar and
pestle together with the coarse salt, and stir
into the yogurt cucumber mixture. Season the
cucumber soup with salt and pepper, cover and
leave to chill in the fridge for 4 hours.

4 Beat the cucumber soup with a hand mixer
until frothy, pour into glasses, and garnish
with grated cucumber and lemon slices
(optional).

Pasties
with Vegetable Filling

*Making these small pasties requires a certain amount
of skill, but it is easily acquired and worth the effect*

Ingredients

1 onion

3 carrots · 2 zucchini

1/2 pound mushrooms

1/3 cup olive oil

4 tablespoons chopped parsley

salt · freshly ground pepper

4 sheets yufka (or puff) pastry

1 tablespoon sherry vinegar

vegetable oil, to brush the
pasties and the baking sheet

parsley leaves, dill sprigs
and onion rings, to garnish

Preparation

SERVES 4

1 Peel the onion and dice finely. Prepare the carrots and
zucchini and peel or wash. Cut both into thin strips. Wash
the mushrooms, dab dry with paper towel and slice thinly.

2 Heat 6 tablespoons olive oil in a large pan and fry the
onions until translucent. Add three quarters of the carrot and
zucchini strips and the mushrooms and fry for about 4 minutes, stirring constantly. Add the parsley and season the
vegetables with salt and pepper.

3 Preheat the oven to 350°F. Cut each sheet of pastry into
3 strips lengthwise and brush the strips with oil. Put
1 tablespoon vegetable filling onto the left end of one strip
of pastry. Now pick up the left corner of the pastry and fold
it diagonally over the filling, forming a triangle. Continue to
fold until the whole strip has been folded into a triangular
packet. Press the ends together.

4 Grease a baking sheet, arrange the pasties on the sheet and
bake for about 12 minutes on the middle rack of the oven
until golden.

5 Meanwhile mix the remaining olive oil with the vinegar and
the remaining strips of vegetable and season generously with
salt and pepper. Serve the salad together with the pasties.
Garnish with herbs and onion rings.

Stuffed Cucumber
with Tuna Cream

Ingredients

2 large cucumbers

2 cans tuna (in brine, about

6 ounces drained weight each)

1 garlic clove

3/4 cup crème fraîche

1/2 teaspoon harissa (see page 9)

3 tablespoons lemon juice

salt · freshly ground pepper

a few sprigs dill

2 tablespoons olive oil

Preparation
SERVES 4

1   Peel the cucumbers, cut into half, and carefully
    hollow out, leaving about an 1/2-inch edge all
    the way around. Allow the tuna to drain in a
    sieve. Peel the garlic. Chop both coarsely.

2   Put the tuna into a high-sided mixing bowl
    together with the crème fraîche, garlic, harissa
    and 1 tablespoon lemon juice, and blend very
    finely with an immersion blender.

3   Season the tuna cream well with salt and
    pepper, and carefully stuff into the hollowed-
    out cucumbers.

4   Wash the dill and shake dry. Pluck the tips of
    the dill from the stems and chop finely. Add to
    the oil, stir with the remaining lemon juice,
    salt and pepper and sprinkle over the stuffed
    cucumbers.

Fried Vegetables
on Garlic Yogurt

Ingredients

1 small eggplant

1 red bell pepper

2 tablespoons olive oil

1 dried red chili pepper

1 teaspoon coriander seeds

salt · freshly ground pepper

2 tablespoons oil

2 teaspoons paprika powder
(extra hot)

1 cup plain whole-milk yogurt

3 garlic cloves

1 tablespoon chopped parsley

Preparation

SERVES 4

1 Prepare and wash the eggplant, cut in half lengthwise. Cut the pepper in half lengthwise, seed and wash. Cut both into thin strips. Heat the olive oil in a pan and sear the vegetable strips in the pan for about 8 minutes over medium heat until light brown, stirring constantly. Remove from the heat.

2 With a pestle and mortar, crush the chili pepper and coriander together with a little salt and pepper and stir into the vegetables.

3 Heat the oil and the paprika powder gradually in a small pan until the oil turns red. Set aside. Mix the yogurt with a little salt. Peel the garlic, press through a garlic press and add to the yogurt.

4 To serve, arrange the yogurt on plates, with the fried vegetables on top. Sprinkle with the paprika oil and parsley. Serve warm, with pita bread (optional).

Boerek Duo
with Cheese and Ground Beef

Turkish "cigars": These delicious small pasties make ideal appetizers and will never cease to provoke admiration

Ingredients

For the goat cheese rolls:

1 bunch each parsley and dill

1 cup goat cheese (feta)

freshly ground pepper

½ teaspoon paprika powder (sweet)

2 sheets yufka (or puff) pastry

1 egg white

For the ground beef packets:

6 ounces tomatoes

1 onion · 1 tablespoon oil

6 ounces lean ground beef

salt · freshly ground pepper

1 tablespoon chopped parsley

2 sheets yufka (or puff) pastry

1 egg white

vegetable oil, for frying

Preparation

MAKES 16 (CHEESE) OR 8 (MEAT)

1 For the goat cheese rolls, wash the herbs and shake dry, pluck the leaves from the parsley stems and the tips of the dill from their stems and chop finely. Crumble the cheese and mix with the herbs, pepper and paprika.

2 Quarter the pastry sheets and cut each quarter in half diagonally. Arrange the cheese filling on top, and turn the edges in slightly. Beat the egg white and brush the edges. Roll the triangles up, starting with the long side.

3 For the mince packets, cut an X into the top and bottom of the tomatoes. Put into boiling hot water for 30 seconds. The skin should come off now. Peel, quarter and seed. Dice the quartered tomatoes finely. Peel the onion and chop finely. Heat the oil in a pan and fry the diced onions until translucent. Add the beef and tomatoes and fry for about 3 minutes. Season with salt and pepper, then stir in the parsley.

4 Quarter the sheets of pastry and arrange the filling on the quarters. Beat the egg white and brush the edges. Fold the pastry sheets to make small packets.

5 Heat the oil in a pan or deep-fryer. Deep-fry the goat cheese rolls and the mince packets, a few at a time, for 3-4 minutes until golden. Remove from the oil, allow to drain on paper towels and serve hot.

Pita Pizza
with Ground Beef

Crunchy and right out of the oven: The Middle East is famous
for its many types of flatbreads, as versatile as Italian pizzas

Ingredients

For the pastry:

1 cake (¾ ounce) compressed

yeast · sugar

3 ¾ cups all-purpose flour

salt

1 tablespoon vegetable oil

2 tablespoons plain yogurt

For the filling:

½ red bell pepper

1 bunch scallions

1 bunch thyme

2 large tomatoes

2 tablespoons oil

about 9 ounces ground lamb

salt · freshly ground pepper

1 tablespoon black caraway

seeds

3 red onions

3 tablespoons chopped parsley

Preparation

MAKES 8

1 For the pastry, preheat the oven to 125°F. Dissolve the yeast in a bowl with ¾ cups lukewarm water. Knead together with the flour, ½ teaspoon salt, the oil and the yogurt to form a smooth dough. Switch off the oven, cover the dough with a dishtowel and let it rise in the oven for about 1 hour.

2 For the filling, seed the pepper, wash and dice finely. Wash the scallions and cut into fine rings. Wash the thyme, shake dry, pluck the leaves from the stems and chop finely. Cut an X into the top and bottom of the tomatoes. Put into boiling hot water for seconds. The skin should come off now. Peel, quarter and seed. Dice the quartered tomatoes finely.

3 Heat the oil in a pan and fry the lamb until crumbly. Season with salt and pepper and set aside. Preheat the oven to 450°F. Line two baking sheets with baking parchment.

4 Knead the dough thoroughly well once more, separate into 8 equal parts and give them the shape of a canoe. Arrange the ground lamb, pepper, scallions and tomatoes on top, leaving the edge free. Sprinkle over with thyme and black caraway seeds, season well with salt and pepper.

5 Fold the edges of the pastry up to keep the filling in place. Arrange the flatbreads on the baking sheets alongside one another and bake (one tray at a time) for about 20 minutes on the middle rack of the oven until golden.

6 Peel the onions, cut into fine rings and mix with the parsley. Serve the pita with the onion-parsley mix.

Vegetarian
Main Dishes

Stuffed Eggplant
with Yogurt Dip

Unbelievably delicious and versatile: Eggplant is quite rightly called the poor man's meat around the Mediterranean

Ingredients

For the eggplant:

4 medium eggplant

2 tablespoons lemon juice

salt · 6 tablespoons olive oil

2 onions · 2 garlic cloves

1 bunch parsley

5 very ripe tomatoes

1 cup cooked rice

1/2 teaspoon ground paprika

(sweet)

freshly ground pepper

cayenne pepper

1/4 teaspoon ground cumin

1 teaspoon sugar

butter for the tray

For the yogurt dip:

2 garlic cloves

1/2 bunch mint

1 cup plain yogurt · salt

freshly ground pepper

Preparation

SERVES 4

1 Prepare the eggplant, wash and cut in half lengthwise. Sprinkle with the lemon juice immediately, then sprinkle with the salt and allow to stand for 30 minutes. Wash off the salt and dab the eggplant dry.

2 In a pan heat 4 tablespoons oil, two at a time, and sear the eggplant halves on both sides for about 5 minutes. Allow to drain on paper towels. With a spoon scrape out the pulp, leaving an edge of about 1/4 inch all the way around. Chop the pulp coarsely.

3 Peel the onions and garlic and dice finely. Wash the parsley and shake dry, pluck the leaves from the stems and chop finely. Cut an X across the top and bottom of 3 tomatoes. Drop them into boiling water for about 1 minute. The skin should come off now. Peel, quarter, seed the tomatoes and dice finely.

4 Heat the remaining oil in a pan and cook the onions and garlic in the pan until translucent. Add the eggplant pulp, the rice, tomatoes, parsley and herbs, and cook for about 4 minutes over low heat until done. Salt to taste.

5 Preheat the oven to 350°F. Place the eggplant shells in a greased casserole dish and fill with the rice-vegetable mixture. Wash the remaining tomatoes and slice finely, removing the thicker stem end. Arrange over the eggplant and sprinkle with salt, pepper and sugar. Bake eggplant for about 35 minutes on the middle rack of the oven until done.

6 For the yogurt dip, peel the garlic and dice finely. Wash the mint and shake dry, pluck off the leaves and chop finely. Stir the yogurt until smooth, mix with the garlic and mint, season to taste with salt and pepper. Serve the stuffed eggplants with the yogurt dip.

Fried Vegetables
with White Beans

This dish can be a meal in itself: While the vegetables are
fried quickly, the spices give them something special

Ingredients

4 scallions

2 small onions

1 small zucchini

4 ounces celeriac

2-3 carrots

1 cup fava beans

(canned)

$1/2$ pound tomatoes

4 tablespoons olive oil

$1/2$ teaspoon ras el hanout

(Moroccan seasoning)

salt · freshly ground pepper

Preparation

SERVES 4

1 Prepare the scallions, wash and cut into large pieces. Peel the onions and cut into larger pieces. Prepare the zucchini, wash and cut into bite-size pieces. Peel the celeriac and carrots, cut the celeriac into small pieces, slice the carrots.

2 Pour the white beans into a sieve and drain. Cut an X across the top and bottom of the tomatoes. Drop them into boiling water for about 1 minute. The skin should come off now. Peel, quarter, seed and chop the tomato quarters coarsely.

3 Heat the oil in a large pan, add the celeriac and carrots and fry for about 3 minutes over medium heat. Add the scallions, the onions and the zucchini and fry for another 3 minutes. Then add the beans and the tomatoes, season to taste with ras el hanout, salt and pepper and cook for another 4 minutes over low heat. Serve the vegetables with couscous or bulgur (optional).

Tip

Ras el hanout is a North African spice mixture consisting of 20 or more spices. Translated, the name means "boss of a grocery store", presumably because all spice merchants produce their own mixture.

Spicy Pancakes
with Spinach and Cheese

Ingredients

4 eggs · salt

2 cups all-purpose flour

¾ cup milk

¾ cup carbonated mineral water

10 ounces leaf spinach (frozen)

1 onion · 1 garlic clove

4 ounces hard cheese

2 tablespoons butter

¼ cup crème fraîche

freshly ground pepper

freshly ground nutmeg

butter for the pan

Preparation
SERVES 4

1 For the pancakes, put the eggs, a pinch of salt, the flour, milk and mineral water into a small bowl and mix into a smooth batter with a hand mixer. Cover and let stand for about 20 minutes.

2 Meanwhile allow the spinach to defrost. Peel the onion and garlic and dice finely. Grate the cheese finely. Melt the butter in a pan and cook the diced onion and garlic until translucent. Add the spinach and fry briefly.

3 Stir in the cheese and crème fraîche, then season the spinach-cheese mixture to taste with salt, pepper and nutmeg.

4 Melt a little butter in a non-stick pan. Fill in a little of the batter, spread over the pan and make a pancake. Make 8 pancakes this way. Spread a little spinach-cheese mix on each pancake, fold the pancakes together, press the sides together firmly and cut into pieces.

Puff Pastry Strudel
with Swiss Chard and Walnuts

Ingredients

1 pound puff pastry (frozen)

1 3/4 pound Swiss chard

1/2 bunch scallions

1 cup goat cheese (feta)

3/4 cup walnuts

6 tablespoons olive oil

1/2 cup butter · 2 eggs

1 teaspoon ground paprika (sweet)

salt · freshly ground pepper

5 tablespoons milk

flour, to dust the working surface

butter for the pan

1 egg yolk

Preparation
SERVES 4

1 Separate the sheets of puff pastry and allow to thaw alongside one another. Prepare the chard, wash and chop coarsely. Clean and wash the scallions, cut into thin rings. Crumble the cheese, chop the walnuts coarsely.

2 Heat 3 tablespoons each oil and butter, cook the scallions and nuts in the butter and oil for 3 minutes. Add the chard and fry all together for 2 minutes, stirring constantly. Allow to cool. Stir in the cheese and 1 egg. Season well with paprika, salt and pepper.

3 Melt the remaining butter, mix with 4 table-spoons milk, the remaining egg and oil. Place the sheets of pastry on top of one another, brushing each sheet with the butter mixture. Roll out on the dusted working surface to a 12-inch x 16-inch rectangle. Preheat the oven to 400°F and grease a baking pan with butter.

4 Spread the chard mixture evenly onto the pastry, roll up to make a strudel and place on the baking pan. Mix the egg yolk with the remaining milk and brush onto the strudel. Bake for about 35 minutes on the middle rack of the oven until golden brown.

Potato Omelet

with Parsley and Turmeric

Here is a simple omelet which makes a nice light meal
on a hot summer's day, or a quick snack at a garden party

Ingredients

8 small potatoes

salt · ½ bunch parsley

8 eggs

½ teaspoon baking powder

½ teaspoon ground turmeric

freshly ground nutmeg

¼ teaspoon ground cinnamon

freshly ground white pepper

½ cup vegetable oil

1 lemon

Preparation

SERVES 4

1 Peel and wash the potatoes, then cook for about 25-30 minutes in salted water until done. Wash the parsley, shake dry, pluck the leaves from the stems and chop finely.

2 Pour the water off the potatoes and allow to drain well. Mash coarsely with a fork while still hot. Allow the potato mixture to cool slightly. Beat the eggs in a bowl. Fold the parsley into the mashed potatoes, and stir in the baking powder. Season the potato-egg mixture with salt, turmeric, nutmeg, cinnamon and pepper to taste.

3 Heat the oil in a large ovenproof pan and pour in the potato-egg mixture. Cover and leave for about 15 minutes at a low temperature, until the edge is golden yellow and the omelet is done in the center.

4 Switch on the grill and cook the omelet under the grill for about 10 minutes until it is golden brown. Remove the omelet from the grill, turn onto paper towels to drain off any excess oil. Wash the lemon under hot water, rub dry and slice. Cut the omelet into pieces and garnish with lemon slices.

Tip

For variation use cilantro instead of the parsley. Serve the omelet with the eggplant paste on page 29, or the sesame dip on page 30.

Spinach Pie
with Goat Cheese

Spicy contents, crunchy casing – this will win over
even those who are not particularly fond of spinach

Ingredients

1 ⅓ cups goat cheese (feta)

1 bunch parsley

1 onion

2 ¼ pounds fresh leaf spinach

salt · freshly ground pepper

freshly ground nutmeg

½ cup melted butter

1 egg

½ cup milk

butter for the pie pan

1 package (about 1 pound)
fillo or yufka pastry sheets

Preparation
SERVES 4

1 Dice the goat cheese finely. Wash the parsley and shake dry, pluck the leaves from the stems and chop finely. Peel the onions and dice finely.

2 Clean the spinach, rinse and place in a pan with just the water clinging to the leaves. Cook over high heat until just wilted. Drain in a sieve and allow to cool. Press out a bit of the excess moisture, chop coarsely, and mix with the diced cheese, onion and parsley. Season with salt, pepper and nutmeg.

3 Melt the butter in a pan, but do not brown. Allow to cool slightly. Beat the egg in a bowl. Then stir in first the milk, then the melted butter.

4 Grease a rectangular pie pan (about 7-inch x 12-inch). Layer half the sheets of pastry in the pan, overlapping slightly, and brush each sheet with a little egg mixture. Arrange the cheese-spinach mixture on top, cover with the remaining sheets of pastry, again brushing each sheet with the egg mixture.

5 Sprinkle the remaining egg mixture over the pie. Put into a cold oven, bake for about 40 minutes at 400°F on the bottom rack of the oven until the pastry is crisp and golden brown. Cut into portions and serve hot or cold.

Zucchini Couscous
with Mushrooms

Ingredients

4 scallions

2 garlic cloves

11 ounces zucchini

7 ounces small mushrooms

1 tablespoon olive oil

$\frac{1}{2}$ cup instant couscous

1 $\frac{1}{2}$ tablespoon yellow curry paste

1 $\frac{2}{3}$ cup vegetable stock

4 sprigs each basil and parsley

salt · cayenne pepper

2 tablespoons lemon juice

Preparation

SERVES 4

1 Wash and prepare the scallions and slice finely. Peel the garlic and dice finely. Wash and prepare the zucchini, cut in half lengthwise and cut into thin slices. Wash the mushrooms and rub dry with paper towels, then also slice finely.

2 Heat the oil in a large pan, add the scallions and garlic and cook. Add the zucchini and mushrooms and fry everything for 3-4 minutes.

3 Stir in the couscous and curry paste and pour in the stock. Cover and leave to simmer at a low temperature for 5-6 minutes, stirring occasionally.

4 Wash the basil and parsley, then shake dry. Pluck the leaves from the stems, chop finely and mix into the zucchini couscous. Season with salt, cayenne pepper and lemon juice.

Couscous
with Mixed Vegetables

Ingredients

2 ⅓ cups instant couscous · salt

3 small zucchini · 4 tomatoes

1 cup pumpkin flesh

1 small eggplant

⅔ cup green beans

½ cup shredded white cabbage

2 garlic cloves

1 dried chili pepper

3 tablespoons vegetable oil

pinch of saffron powder

1 cup vegetable stock

½ cup chickpeas (canned)

freshly ground pepper

cilantro leaves, to garnish

Preparation
SERVES 4

1 Put the couscous into a bowl and pour in 1 ¾ cups lightly salted, boiling water. Leave to swell for 5 minutes. Fluff up the couscous with a fork and keep warm.

2 Trim the zucchini, then rinse and cut into thick sticks. Rinse, halve, seed and chop the tomatoes. Wash the eggplant, and cut it together with the pumpkin flesh into bite-size pieces. Trim and wash the green beans. Cut the cabbage into slices and shred.

3 Peel the garlic and dice finely. Crush the chili pepper in a mortar with a pestle. Heat the oil in a pan and fry the pumpkin, beans and white cabbage in the pan for about 4 minutes. Add the zucchini and eggplant, cover and fry gently for another 4 minutes.

4 Dissolve the saffron in the hot stock, and add to the vegetables. Pour off the chickpeas and allow to drain, then add along with the tomatoes. Cover the vegetables and simmer for another 5 minutes. Season to taste with salt and pepper. Serve on plates with the couscous. Garnish with the cilantro leaves.

Pumpkin and Spinach
with Apricots and Saffron

An unusual combination: The blend of vegetables,
dried apricots and exquisite spices adds variety to any meal

Ingredients

1 3/4 pounds pumpkin

1 3/4 pounds spinach

salt · 3 onions

3 garlic cloves

3 tomatoes

2/3 cup dried apricots

10 saffron threads

3-4 tablespoons olive oil

freshly ground pepper

1/2-1 teaspoon harissa

(see page 9)

1/2 teaspoon ground

cinnamon

1 bunch parsley

Preparation

SERVES 4

1 Peel the pumpkin, seed and cut into bite-size pieces. Clear the spinach, allow to drain and remove large stems. Boil the spinach for 1-2 minutes in a little salted water. Pour into a sieve, rinse with cold water and allow to drain well.

2 Peel the onions and garlic and dice finely. Wash the tomatoes, quarter and seed. Dice the tomato quarters finely. Cut the apricots into small pieces. Dissolve the saffron in 1/2 cup hot water.

3 Heat the oil in a pan, add the onions and garlic and fry gently until translucent. Add the pieces of pumpkin and fry for a few minutes. Pour in the saffron water, add the tomatoes and apricots and season the vegetables to taste with salt, pepper, harissa and cinnamon. Cover the vegetables and cook for about 10 minutes over low heat until the pumpkin is tender but not soft. Stir in the spinach and heat.

4 Wash the parsley and shake dry, pluck the leaves from the stems, chop finely and stir into the pumpkin-spinach vegetables. Season to taste again. Serve with couscous or bulgur (optional).

Tip

As an alternative to dried apricots, add dried dates to the pumpkin-spinach vegetables instead. Or stir in some chopped roasted almonds.

Fennel and Zucchini
with Aniseed

*Two that go together well: Fennel has enough flavor
of its own, but aniseed makes a pleasant addition*

Ingredients

6 fennel bulbs

6 zucchini

5 tablespoons olive oil

1 1/2 tablespoons aniseed

3 tablespoons butter

salt

freshly ground white pepper

star anise, to garnish

Preparation

SERVES 4

1 Wash and prepare the fennel, cut into thin strips. Wash the zucchini and dice.

2 Heat 3 tablespoons oil in a pan and sweat the fennel in the oil over medium heat. Cover and cook for about 20 minutes over low heat until done, stirring occasionally.

3 Heat the remaining oil in a second pan, add the zucchini and fry over medium heat for about 5 minutes (it should not turn brown), stirring constantly. Mix the zucchini with the aniseed into the fennel, and cook the vegetables without a lid for another 10 minutes over medium heat until done.

4 Remove the vegetables from the heat and stir in the butter. Season the vegetables well with salt and pepper. To serve, arrange on plates and garnish with star anise.

Tip

Served alone, with pita bread or with couscous, this dish is perfect for those hot days of summer. It is also an ideal and light side dish for grilled meat or fish.

Chickpea Vegetables
with Couscous and Corn

Ingredients

1 1/4 cups dried chickpeas

2 carrots

2 cups green beans

1 onion · 2 garlic cloves

3 tablespoons olive oil

1 cup vegetable stock

1 1/3 cups peas (frozen)

3 tablespoons raisins

2 1/3 cups instant couscous

salt · freshly ground pepper

2 tablespoons white wine vinegar

3 1/2 ounces corn (canned)

2 tablespoons almonds (coarsely chopped)

Preparation

SERVES 4

1 Allow the chickpeas to soak overnight in cold water. Pour off the water, rinse with cold water and allow to drain. Clean and prepare the carrots, dice finely. Prepare the beans, wash and cut into pieces.

2 Peel the onion and garlic, cut the onion into thin slices, dice the garlic finely. Sweat the strips of onion with oil in a pan until translucent. Add the chickpeas, garlic and stock, bring to a boil, then cover and simmer for 20 minutes over low heat.

3 Add the carrots, beans, peas and raisins and cook for another 15 minutes. Add a little more stock if necessary.

4 Meanwhile cover the couscous with 1 2/3 cups boiling salted water and allow to stand for about 5 minutes.

5 Season the vegetables to taste with salt, pepper and vinegar. Drain the corn in a sieve and mix with the almonds. Fluff up the couscous with a fork and serve on plates. Arrange the vegetables on top. Serve with pita bread (optional).

Brown Lentils
with Tomato Spinach

Ingredients

2 cups small brown lentils

2 onions

2 tablespoons olive oil

2 tablespoons coarsely ground
wheat

1 1/2 cups milk

1 vegetable cube

1 pound leaf spinach

2 garlic cloves

4 ounces tomato

salt · freshly ground pepper

1 tablespoon chopped parsley

Preparation
SERVES 4

1 Rinse the lentils in a sieve, bring to a boil with 4 cups of water and cook for about 45 minutes. Pour into a sieve, allow to drain and keep warm.

2 Meanwhile peel one onion and dice finely. Heat 1 tablespoon oil in a pan and fry the diced onion in the pan until clear. Add the wheat and fry together quickly. Add the milk and vegetable cube, cover the wheat and simmer for about 45 minutes over low heat.

3 Wash the spinach and remove large stems. Peel the second onion and the garlic and dice finely. Cut an X across the top and bottom of the tomatoes and drop into boiling hot water for 30 seconds. The skin should come off now. Peel, quarter, seed and chop the tomatoes coarsely.

4 Fry the onions and garlic in the oil until translucent. Add the spinach and allow to wilt. Add the tomatoes, season with salt and pepper, cover and allow to cook for about 10 minutes. Arrange the lentils and tomato spinach on plates, sprinkle with the wheat sauce and garnish with the parsley.

Spiced Millet
on a Bed of Vegetables

*With this dish made from healthy cereal, crunchy
vegetables and exotic spices, who would still miss their meat?*

Ingredients

1 ¼ cups millet

1 onion

3 garlic cloves

4 tablespoons olive oil

4 tablespoons almond slivers

2 cups vegetable stock

½ cup raisins

½ cinnamon stick

½ teaspoon ground cumin

pinch of saffron powder

salt · freshly ground pepper

1 eggplant

1 leek

1 celery stick

1 medium carrot

Preparation

SERVES 4

1 Rinse the millet in a sieve with lukewarm water and allow to
drain well. Peel the onion and garlic and dice finely. Heat
2 tablespoons oil in a pan and gently fry the diced onion and
garlic in the pan until translucent.

2 Stir in the almonds and millet and roast briefly. Add the
stock, raisins and cinnamon. Season with cumin, saffron,
salt and pepper, cover and leave for about 25 minutes over
very low heat.

3 Meanwhile wash and prepare the eggplant. Cut into 4 lengthwise, then slice into ½-inch slices. Sprinkle with 1 teaspoon
salt and allow to stand for 30 minutes.

4 Wash and prepare the leek and celery, wash and peel the carrots. Cut the vegetables into rings or slices. Rinse the slices
of eggplant and dab dry with paper towels. Heat the remaining oil in a large pan and fry the eggplant well on both sides.
Remove and set aside.

5 Fry the remaining vegetables in the pan briefly, stirring constantly, and add 5 tablespoons water. Cover the vegetables
and simmer gently for about 5 minutes until fork tender. Add
the eggplant slices again, then season the vegetables to
taste with salt and pepper.

6 Arrange the vegetables on plates and sprinkle the spiced millet on top. Garnish with cinnamon sticks (optional).

Saffron Potatoes
with Scallions

*With a delightful medley of a flowors this dish is guaranteed
to turn the humble potato into a star performer*

Ingredients

about 2 1/2 pounds small
potatoes

1 bunch scallions

1 bunch cilantro

3 tablespoons olive oil

2 tablespoons butter

1 bay leaf

1-2 teaspoons cumin seeds

10 saffron threads

salt · freshly ground pepper

Preparation

SERVES 4

1 Preheat the oven to 400°F. Peel and wash the potatoes. Clean and wash the scallions and cut into pieces. Wash the cilantro and shake dry, pluck the leaves from the stems.

2 Heat the oil and butter in a large ovenproof dish, add the potatoes and scallions and sear them on all sides. Add about 2 cups hot water, the bay leaf, cumin, saffron and the plucked cilantro leaves. Season to taste with salt and pepper, cover and cook for about 30 minutes in the oven.

3 Remove the lid and cook the potatoes for another 20 minutes until done and the water has almost evaporated. Season the saffron potatoes once more with salt and pepper.

Tip

Serve the saffron potatoes with the carrot salad on page 19. The potatoes are also a great side dish with grilled meat or fish.

Main Dishes with Meat and Fish

Chermoula Chicken
with Peppers and Eggplant

Culinary greetings from Morocco: The marinade made with peppers and cumin makes the chicken both tender and tasty

Ingredients

1 onion · 4 garlic cloves

¹/₂ cup olive oil

6 tablespoons lemon juice

1 teaspoon ground paprika (sweet)

1 teaspoon ground cumin

salt · freshly ground pepper

4 boneless chicken breasts

1 small eggplant (about 7 ounces)

2 small red and 2 small yellow bell peppers · 2 bay leaves

¹/₂ pound green beans

1 tablespoon butter

Preparation

SERVES 4

1 For the chermoula marinade, peel the onion and garlic. Chop the onion finely, slice the garlic. Mix both with oil, lemon juice, ground paprika and cumin, season with salt and pepper. Wash the chicken, dab dry and brush with half the marinade. Allow to stand for about 30 minutes.

2 Prepare the eggplant, wash and cut lengthwise into thin slices. Quarter the peppers lengthwise, seed and wash. Mix the vegetables with the remaining marinade and the halved bay leaves and also allow to stand for about 30 minutes.

3 Preheat the oven to 400°F. Arrange the chicken and the vegetables in a baking pan (dish) and cook for about 25 minutes on the middle rack of the oven until done.

4 Prepare the beans, wash and cook in boiling salted water until they are tender. Pour into a sieve, rinse with cold water and allow to drain. Just before serving, melt the butter in a pan, toss the beans in the butter and heat. Season with salt and pepper. Arrange the chicken breast and vegetables on plates.

Tip

Add cilantro leaves to give the chermoula marinade stronger flavoring. Wash 1 bunch cilantro and shake dry, pluck the leaves from the stems, chop finely and mix in.

Vegetable Couscous
with Chicken

*Mountains of couscous crowned with chicken and vegetables are
always a delight for the eyes when served at Moroccan homes*

Ingredients

1 ²/₃ cups instant couscous

salt

3 chicken breast portions

2 onions · 1 garlic clove

2 tablespoons vegetable oil

4 tomatoes

2 small zucchini

1 ¹/₂ cups chickpeas (canned)

freshly ground pepper

1 cup vegetable stock

Preparation

SERVES 4

1 Preheat the oven to 350°F. Cover the couscous in a bowl with 1 ¹/₄ cups boiling salted water and allow to swell for 5 minutes. Wash the chicken, dab dry and cut into bite-size pieces. Peel the onions and garlic and chop coarsely.

2 Heat the oil in a pan, sear the chicken in the oil on both sides and set aside on a plate. Fry the onions and garlic in the remaining oil until translucent.

3 Wash, quarter, and seed the tomatoes, then chop coarsely. Wash the zucchini, quarter lengthwise and cut into thick slices. Drain the chickpeas in a sieve.

4 Fluff up the couscous with a fork, mix with the chicken and vegetables. Season with salt and pepper, fill into a casserole or Tajine dish, and cover with the stock. Bake for about 25 minutes on the middle rack of the oven until done.

Tip

Tajines (or tegines) which combine meat with vegetables or fruit, are part of Moroccan high cuisine. The name derives from the clay pot with a conical lid in which stews are traditionally cooked over a fire.

Chicken Tajine
with Salted Lemons

This is one of the most popular tajines: Simmering the chicken in the saffron sauce gives it an especially delicate flavor

Ingredients

1 chicken (about 2 1/2 pounds, cut into 8 pieces)

salt · freshly ground pepper

3 1/2 ounces green olives (pitted)

1 1/2 salted lemons (see page 9)

1 onion

3 garlic cloves

10 threads saffron

4 tablespoons butter

2 tablespoons olive oil

1 teaspoon ground ginger

2 tablespoons each chopped cilantro and parsley

Preparation

SERVES 4

1 Wash the chicken pieces, dab dry and season with salt and pepper. Cook the olives for 30 seconds in boiling hot water. Pour into a sieve, rinse quickly with cold water and allow to drain. Remove the pulp and the seeds of the salted lemons. Wash the lemons, dab dry and cut into thick slices.

2 Peel the onion and garlic and dice finely. Dissolve the saffron threads in 1/3 cup hot water. Heat the butter and the oil in a roasting pan and cook the diced onion until translucent. Add the chicken pieces and fry on both sides.

3 Add the garlic, ginger, dissolved saffron and 1 2/3 cups water and bring everything to a boil. Reduce the heat, cover and leave to simmer for about 1 hour, turning the meat occasionally so that it soaks up the sauce. Add more water if required.

4 Add the olives and lemons, cover and allow to simmer for another 15 minutes. Stir in the herbs and season the sauce with salt and pepper. If the sauce is too thin, remove the chicken and cook the sauce briefly to reduce the quantity. Serve the chicken Tajine with couscous (optional).

Tip

Lemons preserved in salt and lemon juice lend a unique and distinctive flavor to Moroccan dishes. They take about 4 weeks to mature and can last a year (see page 9).

Duck Confit Tajine
with Glazed Pears

Ingredients

4 pieces duck confit (marinated
ducks, store-bought)

15 figs (fresh or canned)

1/2 cup butter

1/2 cup brown sugar

3 pears (peeled and quartered)

a little ground cinnamon

4 onions (finely diced)

1/2 cup chicken stock

3 carrots (sliced) · salt

Preparation
SERVES 4

1 Cover the duck in a pan and heat for about
   10 minutes over low heat in order to melt the
   fat. Allow to drain well and reserve the fat.

2 Wash the figs, then quarter 4 figs and set aside.
   Dice the remaining figs. Melt 1/4 cup butter in a
   pan, add 1/4 cup sugar and allow to caramelize.
   Add the pears, turn in the caramel and dust
   with cinnamon. Put the onions and 2 tablespoons butter into a pan, cover and allow to
   cook for 10 minutes, stirring occasionally.

Add the diced figs and stock and gently
simmer over low heat to reduce.

3 Cover the carrots in a pan with water and add
   the remaining butter, 2 tablespoons sugar and
   1/4 teaspoons salt. Cook the carrots until done
   or until the water has completely evaporated.
   Heat 3 tablespoons duck fat, add the quartered
   figs, sprinkle with sugar and cinnamon and
   fry for about 2 minutes on all sides, sprinkling
   with sugar and cinnamon once more. Serve
   the duck pieces with fig compote, glazed
   pears and carrots.

Lamb Chops
with Herb Butter

Ingredients

12 lamb chops (with long
rib bones if possible)
salt · freshly ground pepper
1/3 ounce fresh ginger root
2 green cardamom pods
1/2 teaspoon whole allspice
2 dried red chili peppers
1/2 teaspoon ground cinnamon
freshly ground nutmeg
3 tablespoons each clarified
butter and walnut oil
2 garlic cloves
2 tablespoons chopped parsley
1 tablespoon chopped mint

Preparation

SERVES 4

1 Wash the lamb chops, dab dry and clean the
bones. Season the meat with salt and pepper.

2 Peel the ginger and grate finely. Break open
the cardamom pods and crush the seeds along
with the allspice and chili peppers with a pestle
and mortar. Mix with cinnamon and nutmeg.

3 Melt the clarified butter in a small pan with
the walnut oil. Peel the garlic and dice finely,
add to the pan.

4 Stir in the spice mixture. Allow the butter to
become a little frothy. Add parsley and mint,
then take the butter off the heat.

5 Brush both sides of the lamb chops with
some of the herb butter. Place on the grill or
under the grill of the oven. Roast for about
6-8 minutes on either side until both sides
are browned well on the outside, but still pink
inside.

6 Melt the remaining herb butter. Serve the lamb
chops with rice and fresh lemon wedges and
sprinkle with herb butter.

Oriental Casserole
with Couscous

Serve up a feast from 1001 Nights: This casserole is perfect if you want to offer your guests something really special that is easy to prepare

Ingredients

4 chicken legs

1 pound lamb (shoulder)

2 onions · 2 garlic cloves

1/2 celery stick

1/2 pound zucchini · 3 carrots

2 green bell peppers

4 tablespoons olive oil

salt · freshly ground pepper

1/2 tablespoon ground paprika
(sweet) · 1/4 tablespoon ground
paprika (extra hot)

pinch of each ground
cloves and saffron

1 small can chickpeas
(10 ounces drained weight)

1 can peeled tomatoes
(1 pound drained weight)

1 1/4 cups instant couscous

1 cup chicken stock

4 tablespoons butter

Preparation

SERVES 4

1 Wash the chicken legs, dab dry and halve at the joint. Cut the lamb into 1-inch cubes.

2 Peel the onion and garlic and dice finely. Clean the celery and zucchini, clean and peel the carrots. Cut the vegetables into chunky pieces. Cut the peppers in half lengthwise, seed, wash and cut into strips.

3 Heat the oil in a large roasting pan and sear the diced lamb well on all sides over medium heat. Remove and set aside on a plate. Sear the chicken legs in the remaining oil. Add the onions and garlic and fry over medium heat for 5 minutes. Return the lamb to the pan, season everything with salt, pepper, ground paprika, cloves and saffron.

4 Pour the chickpeas into a sieve and allow to drain. Add to the meat together with the tomatoes and their juice, the vegetables and 4 cups of water. Cover and simmer for about 1 hour over medium heat.

5 Just before the end of the cooking time, put the couscous into a bowl, cover with hot stock and allow to swell for about 5 minutes. Fluff up with a fork. Melt the butter in a pan over medium heat and warm the couscous in this, again fluffing up with a fork. Increase the temperature and allow the moisture to evaporate.

6 Arrange the couscous on a plate surrounded with the meat and vegetables and pour the sauce over it. Serve with raisins and chili dip (optional).

Lamb Ragout
with Dried Fruit

Tajines of meat and fruit are festive dishes cooked
for happy occasions and have a long culinary tradition

Ingredients

1 1/2 pounds lamb (shoulder)

1/2 cup raisins

1 pound small onions

2 garlic cloves

3 cups dried fruit (e.g.

apricots, dates, prunes)

4 tablespoons olive oil

2 2/3 cups vegetable stock

1 teaspoon ground turmeric

salt · freshly ground pepper

1/2 teaspoon each ground

saffron and cinnamon

2 tablespoons coarsely

chopped pistachios

Preparation
SERVES 4

1 Remove the fat and sinews from the lamb's shoulder and cut the meat into thin slices. Soak the raisins in a little hot water. Peel the onion and garlic. Cut 7 ounces onions into 1/2-inch cubes, quarter the remaining onions. Dice the garlic finely. Chop 3 1/2 ounces dried fruit.

2 Heat the oil in a large pan. Sear the lamb, diced onion and garlic in the pan, stirring constantly. Add 1 2/3 cups stock and season well with turmeric, salt and pepper. Add the chopped dried fruit, cover and simmer for 40 minutes over low heat.

3 Remove the lid, add the remaining dried fruit and the quartered onions. Simmer for another 15-20 minutes in the open pan.

4 Pour the raisins into a sieve, allow to drain and add together with the remaining stock. Season the ragout with saffron, cinnamon, salt and pepper and simmer for another 5 minutes over low heat. Season to taste once more. Arrange the lamb ragout on plates, sprinkle with pistachios and serve with couscous or pita bread (optional).

Tip

There are two types of raisins: sultanas, which are dried large and seedless grapes, in golden or brown color, and currants, which are small dried, blackish blue grapes.

Leg of Lamb
with Curry Sauce

Ingredients

4 legs of lamb (about ¹/₂ pound

each) · salt

freshly ground pepper

2 carrots · 1 celery stick

1 leek · 2 onions

2 garlic cloves

4 tablespoons clarified butter

2 bay leaves

2 sprigs each thyme and

rosemary

1 ²/₃ cups dry white wine

1 ²/₃ cups lamb stock

4 ounces each dried apricots and

prunes · ²/₃ cup light cream

1-2 tablespoons curry powder

Preparation

SERVES 4

1 Remove as much of the fat from the legs as
   possible, season with salt and pepper. Peel or
   wash carrots, celery, leek, onions and garlic,
   and cut into pieces.

2 Preheat the oven to 300°F. Heat the clarified
   butter in a roasting pan, sear the leg of lamb
   in the fat on all sides, then remove from the
   pan and set aside. Put the vegetables, the bay
   leaves and the herbs into the roasting pan.
   Add the wine and simmer until the juices are

almost evaporated. Add the lamb stock and the
legs, cover and cook for about 2 ¹/₂ hours on
the middle rack of the oven. Add a little more
water or stock if necessary.

3 Soak the dried fruit in lukewarm water. Remove
   the cooked meat from the roasting pan, cover
   and leave in a warm place. Put the juices from
   the pan through a sieve, skim off the fat and
   bring to a boil with the drained dried fruit. Add
   cream, stir in the curry powder and reduce for
   about 10 minutes. Season the sauce with salt
   and pepper, and serve with the legs of lamb.

Lamb Couscous
with Raisins and Onions

Ingredients

1 pound lamb

1 ½ pound white onions

3 garlic cloves · ⅔ cup raisins

3 tablespoons olive oil

1 ⅔ cups lamb stock

salt · freshly ground pepper

½ bunch cilantro leaves

1 ⅓ cups instant couscous

1 ¾ cups vegetable stock

1 tablespoon butter

1 tablespoon brown sugar

½ teaspoon each harissa
(see page 9), ground
cinnamon and paprika (sweet)

Preparation

SERVES 4

1 Cut the lamb into bite-size cubes. Peel the onions and garlic. Dice one third of the onions and the garlic finely, cut the remaining onions into segments. Soak the raisins in hot water for 30 minutes, then pour into a sieve and allow to drain.

2 Heat 2 tablespoons oil in a pan, add the lamb, diced onion and garlic, then sear. Add the stock and season with salt and pepper. Add the cilantro leaves, cover and cook for 50 minutes until done.

3 Cover the couscous in a bowl with 1 cup boiling hot stock and leave for about 5 minutes to swell. Fluff up with a fork, then keep in a warm place until serving.

4 Heat the remaining oil and butter in a pan and add the sugar to caramelize. Add the onion segments and roast until light brown, stirring constantly. Pour in the raisins and the remaining stock. Season the raisin onions with harissa, cinnamon, paprika, salt and pepper and simmer for another 4 minutes. Serve the couscous with the lamb and the raisin onions.

Lamb Kebabs
with Spinach Salad

*For barbeque fans who like a change: These skewers are
quick to make and satisfy even the most demanding taste buds*

Ingredients

For the salad:

8 ounces baby spinach

1 pomegranate

1/3 cup plain yogurt

3 tablespoons olive oil

salt · freshly ground pepper

cumin powder

For the kebabs:

1/3 ounce fresh ginger root

1 onion

6 tablespoons olive oil

1 1/2 pound ground lamb

2 teaspoons curry powder

1 egg yolk

2 tablespoons chopped parsley

juice of 1 lime

Preparation

SERVES 4

1 To prepare the lamb kebabs, soak 12 long wooden skewers in cold water for about 30 minutes. For the spinach salad, clean the spinach, allow to drain and remove coarse stems. Halve the pomegranate. Remove the seeds with a spoon, catching any juices. Mix the seeds with the juice, yogurt and oil. Season the vinaigrette with salt, pepper and cumin.

2 For the kebabs, peel the ginger root and the onion and chop finely. Heat 2 tablespoons oil in a pan and gently fry the diced onion in the oil until translucent. Mix the ground meat with the diced onion, the ginger, curry, egg yolk and the parsley and season well with salt and pepper.

3 Wet your hands and divide the meat into 12 portions. Press them firmly around the skewers and form into thin oval shapes. Brush the skewers with the remaining oil and roast on the grill (or under the grill of the oven) until golden brown on all sides.

4 Mix the spinach with the yogurt pomegranate vinaigrette. Sprinkle the skewers with the lime juice and serve with the spinach salad.

Tajine of Meatballs
in Tomato Sauce

In the Arab world meatballs are highly regarded and considered
sophisticated: Your guests will find these small spicy balls irresistible

Ingredients

For the sauce:

2 pounds very ripe tomatoes

2 small onions · 2 garlic cloves

3 tablespoons olive oil

1 tablespoon ras el hanout

1 tablespoon tomato paste

1 teaspoon chopped thyme

1 tablespoon chopped parsley

salt · freshly ground pepper

For the meatballs:

2 very dry bread rolls (one day
old) · milk for soaking · 1 small
onion · 2 tablespoons butter

1 pound ground beef · 1 egg

2 tablespoons chopped parsley

salt · freshly ground pepper

clarified butter, for frying

Preparation

SERVES 4

1 For the sauce, prepare the tomatoes, onions and garlic. Cut an X across the top and bottom of the tomatoes, drop them into boiling water for bout 30 seconds and remove the skins, then quarter and seed the tomatoes. Dice the flesh finely. Peel the onions and garlic and dice finely.

2 Heat the oil in a pan and gently fry the onions and garlic until translucent. Stir in the ras el hanout and the tomato paste and cook gently for 2-3 minutes. Add the tomatoes, then cook, stirring frequently, for about 30 minutes until the sauce has thickened. Add the herbs and season the sauce with salt and pepper.

3 For the meatballs, soak the rolls in a little lukewarm milk. Peel the onion and dice finely. Melt the butter in a small pan and cook the onions until translucent. Put the ground beef into a bowl, squeeze out the rolls and mix into the beef, together with the diced onion, the egg and the parsley. Season the mixture to taste with salt and pepper.

4 Wet your hands and form the beef mixture into small balls. Heat the clarified butter in a pan and fry the balls in batches until golden brown on all sides. Heat the beef balls in the tomato sauce briefly and serve with the sauce on plates. Garnish with sour cream and coarsely chopped parsley (optional). Serve with rice or pita bread.

Savory Beef Pie
in Yufka Pastry

Ingredients

1 pound cauliflower · 1 onion

10 1/2 ounces pickled pumpkin (jar)

5 tablespoons pine nuts

3 tablespoons olive oil

1 3/4 pounds ground beef

1/2 cup raisins · salt

cayenne pepper

1/2 teaspoon each ground ginger

and cumin

2 tablespoons chopped parsley

1 1/4 cup soft goat cheese

3 egg yolks

butter for the cake pan

4 sheets yufka pastry

2 tablespoons melted butter

Preparation

SERVES 4–6

1 Prepare the cauliflower, wash and cut into florets. Peel the onion, halve and cut into thin strips. Drain the pumpkin, reserving the pickle juice. Slice the pumpkin pieces. Roast the pine nuts in a pan without oil until golden.

2 Heat the oil in a large pan and fry the beef in the pan until crumbly. Add the strips of onion, pumpkin pieces with pickle juice, raisins, pine nuts and cauliflower, cover and fry gently for about 10 minutes.

3 Season the beef mixture with salt, cayenne pepper, ginger and cumin, stir in the parsley. Blend the goat cheese with the egg yolks and combine with the beef mixture.

4 Preheat the oven to 400°F and grease an 11-inch springform cake pan. Halve the sheets of pastry and arrange in the pan so that they overlap, leaving pastry all around to cover the filling. Fill the ground beef mixture into the pan, cover with the pastry and brush with the melted butter. Bake for about 30 minutes on the middle rack of the oven.

Turkish Kofta
with Oven Potatoes

Ingredients

2 onions · 3 tablespoons olive oil

1/2 bunch parsley

1/4 cup grated hard cheese

1 1/4 pounds ground beef · 1 egg

4 tablespoons breadcrumbs

salt · freshly ground pepper

1 teaspoon each ground cumin

and paprika (sweet)

1 teaspoon dried thyme

1 pound potatoes

1 pound tomatoes

2 tablespoons tomato paste

3/4 cup vegetable stock

4 tablespoons plain yogurt

3 tablespoons lemon juice

Preparation
SERVES 4

1   Peel the onions and dice finely. Heat 1 table-spoon oil and gently fry the onions until translucent. Wash the parsley and shake dry, pluck the leaves from the stems and chop finely. Grate the cheese.

2   Mix the beef with the onions, breadcrumbs, egg, 2 tablespoons chopped parsley, cheese, salt, pepper, cumin, paprika and thyme thoroughly in a bowl. Wet your hands and shape the meat mixture into 12 balls. Preheat the oven to 400°F.

3   Peel the potatoes, wash and quarter. Wash and halve the tomatoes, removing the thick stem. Bring the stock to a boil and stir in the tomato paste. Brush a deep baking pan with the remaining oil. Arrange the meat balls and potatoes in the pan and pour the stock over. Bake for about 30 minutes on the middle rack of the oven until done. After 15 minutes cooking time, add the halved tomatoes.

4   Mix the yogurt with the lemon juice and remaining parsley and season with salt and pepper. Arrange the kofta on plates with potatoes and tomatoes. Serve with yogurt sauce.

Spiced Yellow Rice
with Mussels and Tomatoes

Festive yellow rice – here served with fresh mussels –
is to the Moroccans what paella is to the Spaniards

Ingredients

3 shallots · 2 garlic cloves

2 small tomatoes

1 ½ cups green beans

1 pound mussels

¾ cup basmati rice

5 coriander seeds · 2 cloves

3 grains allspice

2 green cardamom seeds

⅓ cinnamon stick

3 tablespoons olive oil

½ teaspoon each ground
turmeric and paprika (sweet),
plus freshly ground nutmeg

1 ½ cups vegetable stock

salt · freshly ground pepper

1 tablespoon each chopped
cilantro and parsley

Preparation

SERVES 4

1   Peel the shallots and garlic and dice finely. Cut an X across the top and bottom of the tomatoes. Drop them into boiling water for about 30 seconds. The skin should come off now. Peel, quarter and seed the tomatoes. Dice the flesh finely. Trim and wash the beans.

2   Clean the mussels well under cold running water, discarding any open shells. Rinse the rice in a sieve under cold running water until the water is clear, then allow to drain.

3   With a pestle and mortar crush the spices that have not been ground. Heat the oil in a large pan. Gently fry the diced shallots and garlic and all spices until translucent. Add the diced tomatoes and also cook for a few minutes.

4   Add the stock, then the rice, bring to a boil and cook for about 5 minutes over low heat. Add the mussels and beans and simmer for about another 15 minutes. Remove the pan from the heat, allow the rice to swell for about another 10 minutes. Season with salt and pepper and stir in the herbs.

Tip

If mussels are not your favorite food, you can also prepare the spiced yellow rice with fish, using 8-10 ounces diced fillet of white fish and adding it to the rice after about 12 minutes cooking time.

Sea Bream
in an Almond Crust

Ingredients

1 ²/₃ pounds small waxy potatoes

¹/₄ teaspoon ground saffron · salt

4 small sea breams (about

³/₄ pound each)

2 tablespoons lemon juice

freshly ground pepper

1 bunch cilantro

oil for the baking pan

4 tablespoons olive oil

1 cup ground almonds

3 tablespoons sugar

2 teaspoons ground cinnamon

3 tablespoons rosewater

1 garlic clove · 1 egg

Preparation
SERVES 4

1 Peel the potatoes, wash and cook with the saffron for about 15 minutes in salted water. Rinse the fish both inside and out under cold running water, dab dry, and season with lemon juice, salt and pepper. Wash the cilantro, shake dry and put it inside the fish. Grease a deep baking pan and arrange the fish on it.

2 Drain the saffron potatoes and toss in 2 tablespoons hot oil. Arrange on the baking pan around the fish.

3 Preheat the oven to 400°F. Mix the almonds with the sugar, cinnamon and rosewater in a bowl. Peel the garlic and dice finely, then blend in with the remaining oil and the egg. Add a little cold water and stir until the almond mixture is smooth.

4 Spread the almond paste over the fish, omitting the heads and tails. Bake the fish for 25-35 minutes on the middle rack of the oven until the crust is lightly brown. Serve the sea bream with the saffron potatoes on warmed plates.

Marinated Salmon
in a Coat of Sesame

Ingredients

1 garlic clove

juice of 2 limes

1/3 cup olive oil

2 tablespoons sesame oil

1 tablespoon chopped thyme

1/2 teaspoon baharat (hot
Arabian spice mixture)

salt · freshly ground pepper

2 pounds skinless salmon fillet

5-6 tablespoons each white and
black sesame seeds

Preparation

SERVES 4

1 Peel and dice the garlic finely. Mix with the lime juice, the olive oil, sesame oil, thyme and baharat. Season the marinade with salt and pepper. Wash the salmon fillet, dab dry with paper towels and brush with the marinade. Cover and leave in the fridge for 2-3 hours.

2 Preheat the oven to 400°C. Mix the two types of sesame seeds on a flat plate. Dab the salmon slightly dry, cut into portions and toss in the sesame seeds.

3 Arrange the salmon pieces in a casserole dish and bake for about 20 minutes on the middle rack of the oven. Garnish with lemon slices or wedges (optional). Serve with the orange salad on page 18.

Tuna Steaks
with Paprika Sauce

A good catch all round: This aromatic fish is available all year round and has found an ideal companion in the hot garlic sauce

Ingredients

1 yellow and 1 red bell pepper

2 red chili peppers

1 pound ripe tomatoes

2 white onions

3 garlic cloves

1 teaspoon each whole allspice seeds and cumin seeds

4 tuna steaks (4 ounces each)

salt · freshly ground pepper

3 tablespoons clarified butter

1 teaspoon ground ginger

1 3/4 ounces tomato paste

1/2 bunch parsley

cayenne pepper

Preparation

SERVES 4

1 Cut the bell peppers and chili peppers in half lengthwise, seed and wash. Dice the bell peppers finely, cut the chili peppers into thin strips. Cut an X across the top and bottom of the tomatoes. Drop them into boiling water for about 30 seconds. The skin should come off now. Peel, quarter and seed the tomatoes. Dice the flesh finely.

2 Peel the onions and garlic, cut the onions into small strips, dice the garlic finely. Crush the allspice and cumin with a pestle and mortar.

3 Wash the tuna steaks, dab dry and season with salt and pepper. Heat the clarified butter in a pan and sear the steaks for about 1 minute at a medium temperature on each side. Remove and reserve on a plate.

4 Gently fry the onions and garlic in the remaining butter until translucent. Add the peppers and chilies and fry further. Add the tomatoes and spices; fry everything together for another 5 minutes, stirring constantly. Stir in 2/3 cup water and the tomato paste and allow the sauce to simmer over low heat for about 10 minutes.

5 Wash the parsley and shake dry, pluck the leaves from the stems, chop finely and mix into the sauce. Put the tuna steaks into the sauce, season with salt, pepper and cayenne pepper. Cover and allow to stand for another 5 minutes.

6 Arrange the tuna steaks with the paprika sauce on plates. Serve with pita bread (optional) and garnish with deep-fried whole parsley or fine bell pepper strips.

Spinach Pilaf
with Prawns and Currants

Ingredients

1 bunch parsley · 2 onions

4 garlic cloves · 7 tablespoons butter

2 teaspoons black pepper corns

(whole) · 1/2 teaspoon each

coriander and cumin seeds

1/2 teaspoon dried thyme

2 teaspoons dried mint

1 teaspoon coarse salt

1 1/3 cups short-grain rice (e.g.

Arborio) · 1 pound 5 ounces leaf

spinach (frozen) · 2 1/2 cups chick-

en stock · 4 tablespoons currants

1 pound fresh or frozen jumbo

prawns (ready-to-cook)

salt · freshly ground pepper

Preparation
SERVES 4

1 Wash the parsley, shake dry, pluck the leaves
from the stems and chop finely. Peel the onions
and garlic and dice finely. Melt 4 tablespoons
butter in a roasting pan and sweat the diced
onion and half the garlic in the butter with
the parsley.

2 Crush the spices, dried herbs and the salt with
a pestle and mortar. Add to the pan and sear
briefly. Add the rice and fry gently until translucent, stirring constantly.

3 Add the frozen spinach, the stock and the
currants. Cover and simmer for about 25 minutes over low heat until the rice is done.

4 Wash the prawns and dab dry. Melt the
remaining butter in a pan and fry the prawns
for about 5 minutes on both sides with the
remaining garlic. Season with salt and pepper.
Stir the spinach pilaf with a spoon, then serve
on plates with the prawns, or in small bowls.
Sprinkle with lemon juice (optional).

Sea Bass
with Walnut Filling

Ingredients

2 large sea bass (about 1 1/2
pound each, ready-to-cook)

salt · 2 garlic cloves

6 tablespoons olive oil

1 green bell pepper

3 shallots

8 tablespoons chopped walnuts

1/2 pomegranate

1 teaspoon chopped parsley

freshly ground pepper

butter for the pan

Preparation

SERVES 4

1 Wash the fish both inside and out, dab dry and
cut lengthwise along the outside of both sides
to the bones. Salt both inside and out. Peel
the garlic, dice finely and mix with the oil.
Brush the fish with half the garlic oil.

2 Cut the bell pepper in half lengthwise, seed,
wash and dice finely. Peel the shallots, dice
finely and cook in a little garlic oil until
translucent. Add the pepper and coarsely
chopped walnuts, and roast for 3 minutes.

3 Seed the pomegranate with a spoon. Add the
shiny ruby seeds to the nut mixture together
with the parsley. Season with salt and pepper.

4 Preheat the oven to 425°F. Stuff the sea bass
with the nut mixture and secure with wooden
skewers.

5 Grease a deep baking pan and place the fish
in it. Cook for about 30 minutes in the oven,
brushing with the remaining garlic oil. Serve
with the sesame dip on page 30 (optional).

Desserts
and Drinks

Sweet Couscous
with Oranges and Pomegranate

It doesn't always have to be savory: With a mix of fruits and almonds couscous even makes a good dessert

Ingredients

4 tablespoons raisins

4 dried apricots

4 dried prunes

1 pomegranate

3 tablespoons flaked almonds

1 orange

1 1/2 cups instant couscous

salt · 3 tablespoons butter

2 tablespoons orange-
blossom water

2 teaspoons ground cinnamon

3 tablespoons sugar

Preparation

SERVES 4

1 Cover the raisins in a bowl with hot water and allow to swell for 30 minutes. Cut the dried fruit into small pieces. Halve the pomegranate, remove the seeds with a spoon and discard the pith. Roast the almond flakes in a skillet without oil until golden.

2 Peel the orange, removing also the white pith. Lift the fruit segments out from their membranes, catching any juice.

3 Cover the couscous with 1 1/4 cup boiling hot water, season with 1 pinch of salt and allow to swell for about 5 minutes. Fluff up with a fork and stir in the butter.

4 Pour the raisins into a sieve and allow to drain. Mix with the dried fruit, pomegranate seeds, orange slices, sliced almonds, orange juice and orange-blossom water into the couscous.

5 Season the couscous with 1 teaspoon cinnamon and the sugar. Arrange on plates or in small bowls, and dust with the remaining cinnamon.

Tip

There is more bite to this dessert if, instead of sliced almonds, you use 2 tablespoons roasted almond slivers as well as 1 tablespoon each pistachio and pine nuts.

Fig Pastries
with Vanilla Sauce

These heavenly crisp pastries combined with a creamy sauce are easily addictive. They are prepared to mark special occasions

Ingredients

For the sauce:

1 vanilla pod

2 cups milk

6 egg yolks

1/2 cup sugar

For the pastries:

butter for the sheet

6 figs (about 10 ounces)

6 ounces white almonds

2/3 cup butter

1 1/2 cups brown sugar

1 teaspoon ground cinnamon

4 sheets yufka pastry

confectioner's sugar and ground cinnamon, for dusting

Preparation

MAKES 16

1 For the vanilla sauce, cut the vanilla pod open lengthwise and scrape out the contents with a sharp knife. Bring the milk to a boil with both the vanilla pod and the seeds.

2 Meanwhile whisk the egg yolks and the sugar together in a bowl until pale yellow and creamy. Remove the vanilla pod from the boiling milk and gradually add the vanilla milk to the egg yolk and sugar mixture, stirring constantly. Fill the mixture into a pan, return to the heat and cook gently until the sauce thickens, whisking constantly. Remove from the heat, allow to cool, then set aside in a cold place.

3 Preheat the oven to 350°F. Grease a baking sheet. Wash the dates and dice finely. Roast the almonds without oil in a pan, then chop finely. Melt 1/2 cup butter in a pan, add the sugar and allow to caramelize, stirring constantly, until golden. Stir in the dates, almonds and cinnamon and allow to cook for 2-3 minutes. Remove from the heat and allow to cool.

4 Cut each sheet of pastry into 4 rectangles. Put 1 tablespoon filling at the center of each rectangle. Bring up the corners of the rectangle, over the filling, and fasten together at the center with a small skewer, like a small sack. Melt the remaining butter and brush over the pastry sacks. Arrange on the baking sheet and bake for 3-4 minutes on the middle rack of the oven until golden brown. Remove from the oven and take out the wooden skewers.

5 Arrange the vanilla sauce on plates. Dust the pastries with confectioner's sugar and cinnamon and place in the sauce.

Baklava
with Dates and Nuts

Ingredients

butter for the pan

1 package yufka pastry sheets

(about 1 1/4 pounds)

vegetable oil, for brushing the

pastry sheets

1 1/3 cups shelled hazelnuts

1 cup chopped dates

2 egg whites

1 3/4 cups sugar

2 tablespoons rosewater

1 tablespoon lemon juice

Preparation
SERVES 8–10

1 Preheat the oven to 350°F. Grease a 10-inch spring baking form. Roll each sheet of yufka pastry out separately to fit the form. Brush each sheet of pastry with a little oil and stack the sheets in 2 piles.

2 Grate the hazelnuts coarsely. Cut the dates in half, remove the pits, than chop the halves into pieces. Whisk the egg whites until stiff with 1/2 cup sugar. Stir in the hazelnuts, dates and 1 tablespoon rosewater.

3 Put one stack of pastry in the spring form and arrange the nut-date mixture on top. Cover with the remaining sheets and cut the cake into diamonds about 1 1/2-inch wide with a knife. Bake for about 35 minutes on the middle rack of the oven until golden brown.

4 Bring the remaining sugar to a boil with 3/4 cup water until slightly reduced. Stir in the lemon juice and the remaining rosewater. Pour the syrup over the baklava immediately and allow to cool in the pan.

Semolina Yogurt Cake
with Almonds

Ingredients

butter for the form

$1/2$ cup soft butter (or more)

1 $1/2$ cups confectioner's sugar

grated rind and juice of 1 lemon

3 eggs

3 cups fine semolina

1 teaspoon baking powder

$1/2$ cup plain yogurt

$1/2$ cup ground almonds

1 $3/4$ cups sugar

1 tablespoon lemon juice

confectioner's sugar, for dusting

Preparation

SERVES 8–10

1 Preheat the oven to 350°F and grease a spring-form cake pan. Beat the butter together with the confectioner's sugar, lemon rind, lemon juice and eggs until creamy.

2 Mix the semolina with the baking powder and stir into the egg-butter mixture. Mix the yogurt and almonds and also fold into the mixture. Fill the mixture into the pan, level the surface and bake for about 40 minutes on the middle rack of the oven until golden brown.

3 Meanwhile bring the sugar and lemon juice to a boil with 1 cup water, cook for 2 minutes, then allow to cool. Prick into the slightly cooled cake several times with a wooden skewer and drizzle with the sugar syrup. Cover with plastic wrap and allow to cool.

4 Just before serving, dust the semolina cake with confectioner's sugar and cut into equal pieces. Serve with exotic fruits to taste (e.g. passion fruit and papaya).

Sweet Rice Pudding
with Saffron and Raisins

An incredible transformation: This recipe turns the beloved comfort into an irresistible dessert. Your family will love you for it

Ingredients

½ cup short-grain rice

1 ½ cups milk · salt

butter for the dish

1 tablespoon breadcrumbs

¼ teaspoon saffron powder

2 eggs

2 teaspoons ground cinnamon

1 tablespoon sugar

2 tablespoons chopped almonds

2 tablespoons raisins

Preparation

SERVES 4

1 Rinse the rice in a sieve under running cold water and allow to drain. Bring the milk to a boil with a little salt, add the rice and stir. Cover and simmer until done and the milk is almost completely absorbed. Allow to cool.

2 Preheat the oven to 350°F. Grease a rectangular oven-proof dish or four small oven-proof bowls and dust with breadcrumbs.

3 Dissolve the saffron in a little hot water. Separate the eggs. Whisk the whites in a bowl with a pinch salt until stiff. Whisk the yolks in a second bowl with the saffron, cinnamon and sugar until creamy.

4 Mix the rice with the almonds and raisins. Stir in the egg yolk mixture and fold in the egg whites. Fill the rice mixture into the form or smaller bowls. Sprinkle with sugar, if you like it very sweet.

5 Bake the rice for 20-30 minutes on the middle rack of the oven until golden brown. Serve hot or cold with compote.

Tip

Sprinkle the rice with a little sugar a few minutes before the end of the baking time and switch on the grill for a beautifully caramelized topping.

Pastry Crescents
filled with Almond Paste

These famous Moroccan pastries, best known abroad as
"gazelle's horns", go very well with a cup of coffee or tea

Ingredients

For the pastry:

2 cups all-purpose flour

1/2 cup butter · salt · 1 table-

spoon orange-blossom water

2 egg yolks · flour for the

working surface · 1 egg white

For the filling:

2 tablespoons orange-

blossom water · 1 egg

2/3 cup confectioner's sugar

1 1/3 cups ground almonds

1/2 teaspoon grated orange rind

1/4 teaspoon ground cinnamon

confectioner's sugar for the

working surface

Also:

butter for the baking sheet

orange-blossom water,

for brushing

confectioner's sugar, to dust

Preparation

SERVES ABOUT 35

1 For the pastry, sift the flour into a bowl. Add the butter and a pinch of salt. Mix the orange-blossom water with 1 egg yolk and 4 tablespoons water in a small bowl, add to the butter-flour mixture and knead to a smooth dough. Roll dough into a ball, wrap with plastic wrap and leave for about 30 minutes in a cool place.

2 For the filling, mix the orange-blossom water in a bowl with the egg. Add the confectioner's sugar, almonds, orange rind and cinnamon and knead to a smooth paste.

3 Dust the working surface with confectioner's sugar and form the almond paste into a long roll. Cut into about 35 pieces. Shape each into a 1 1/2-inch roll.

4 Preheat the oven to 400°F. Grease a baking sheet. Dust the working surface with flour and roll out the dough very thinly. With a pastry cutter cut out 3 1/2-inch circles.

5 Place 1 almond roll onto each circle, brush the edge of the pastry with beaten egg white. Fold the pastry together to form half moons and press the edges together firmly. Bend these half moons to make horns.

6 Arrange the pastries on the baking sheet. Mix the remaining egg yolks with a little water and brush over the pastries. Bake for about 15 minutes on the middle reack of the oven. Remove from the oven, allow to cool briefly, brush with orange-blossom water, then dust with confectioner's sugar.

Orange Balouza
with Rosewater

*Fresh, fruity and light – this unusual layered dessert with
honey and rosewater will satisfy even those with a sweet tooth*

Ingredients

For the milk layer:

3 level tablespoons cornstarch

2 cups milk

1 tablespoon rosewater

2 tablespoons honey

For the orange layer:

3 level tablespoons cornstarch

2 cups orange juice (freshly
squeezed)

2 tablespoons honey

For the garnish:

about 1 ounce dark baking
chocolate

orange peel or peel strips

Preparation

SERVES 6

1 For the milk layer, mix the cornstarch with 3 tablespoons of
milk and the rosewater until smooth. Heat the remaining milk
in a pan with the honey. Add the cornstarch, bring to a boil,
stirring constantly until it thickens. Remove the milk mixture
from the heat and allow to cool a little.

2 For the orange layer, mix the cornstarch with 3 tablespoons
orange juice. Heat the remaining orange juice in a pan with
the honey. Add the cornstarch, bring to a boil, stirring
constantly, until it thickens. Remove the orange juice from
the heat and allow to cool a little.

3 Line six small flat bowls (about 7 fluid ounces each) with
plastic wrap. Fill the thickened orange juice into the bowls
and carefully pour the milk cream on top. Allow to set in the
fridge.

4 For the decoration, melt the chocolate in a pan over hot
water. Dip half the orange peel in the liquid chocolate and
allow to dry on waxed paper or baking parchment. Turn the
Balouza out of the bowls onto plates and garnish with the
chocolate peel and remaining orange peel.

Tip

To vary this dish, make the fruit layer out of
mango or passion fruit juice. This gives the
Balouza that special exotic flavor.

Dried Fruit Compote
with Crème Fraîche

Ingredients

10 ounces mixed dried fruit
(e.g. apricots, dates, figs,
prunes, raisins)

1 ounce each peeled almonds,
shelled pine nuts and pistachio
nuts

3 tablespoons sugar

1/3 cup crème fraîche or sour
cream

Preparation

SERVES 4

1 Rinse the dried fruit in a sieve with warm
water, and allow to drain. Put into a pan with
the almonds, pine nuts and pistachios.

2 Sprinkle the sugar over the fruit and nut
mixture and add 1 cup water. Bring to a boil,
cover and simmer gently for about 20 minutes.

3 Remove the pan from the heat and allow the
dried fruit compote to cool. Put into the fridge
to chill for several hours.

4 To serve, arrange the compote on plates. Stir
the crème fraîche until smooth and creamy and
add a few dots as a topping to the compote.
Garnish with mint leaves (optional).

Rice Pudding
with Lychees and Pistachios

Ingredients

¹/₂ cup basmati rice

3 green cardamom pods

scant 2 ¹/₂ cups milk

¹/₂ cup light cream

¹/₂ cup sugar

3 tablespoons butter

pinch saffron powder

¹/₄ cup shelled pistachios

2 tablespoons raisins

2 tablespoons rosewater

lychees, to garnish

Preparation

SERVES 4

1 Rinse the rice in a sieve under cold running water until the water runs clear, allow to drain. Bring to a boil with ³/₄ cup water, cover and simmer for about 10 minutes.

2 Open the cardamom pods and mix the seeds with the milk, cream, sugar, butter and saffron into the rice. Bring to a boil briefly and simmer gently for about 30 minutes, stirring constantly.

3 Chop the pistachios finely. Reserve 1 tablespoon for the garnish, and mix the remainder with the raisins and rosewater into the rice pudding. Fill dessert bowls with the pudding, allow to cool briefly, then put them into the fridge for 2-3 hours.

4 To serve, sprinkle the remaining pistachios over the rice pudding. Peel the lychees and remove the pits. Garnish the rice pudding with the fruit.

Yogurt Cream
with Saffron

An elegant dessert that melts on your tongue: This exquisite saffron cream from Turkey is always worth a second helping

Ingredients

1 1/2 envelopes Knox unflavored
gelatin powder

a few threads saffron

1 cup milk

3 egg yolks

1/2 cup sugar

2/3 cup plain yogurt

Preparation

SERVES 4

1 Bring the milk to a boil in a pan with the saffron, then reduce the temperature.

2 Mix the egg yolks with the sugar and 6 tablespoons saffron milk in a bowl, then gradually stir it into the remaining saffron milk. Whisk the milk until it thickens. Do not allow the mixture to boil, removing the pan from the heat if necessary.

3 Add the gelatin to the cream and let stand for 1 minute. Then stir for 2 minutes until the gelatin is dissolved. Allow the cream to cool in a pan over ice water, stirring constantly, then fold in the yogurt.

4 Fill dessert bowls or glasses with the saffron cream and leave to set in the fridge for about 3 hours. Serve with almond cookies (optional).

Tip

Add variety by using vanilla or apricot yogurt. If you use whipped cream (sweetened if preferred) to fold in instead of yogurt, the result is a wonderfully fluffy cream.

Rice Pudding
with Vanilla Flavor

Sheer temptation for dessert lovers: This delicious rice pudding
takes longer to make, but the result is definitely worth it

Ingredients

1/2 cup short-grain rice

4 cups milk

4 tablespoons light cream

1 cup sugar

1 vanilla pod

3 tablespoons cornstarch

salt

cinnamon powder, to dust

Preparation

SERVES 4

1 Rinse the rice in a sieve under cold running water and allow to drain. Bring the rice to a boil with 2 cups water in a medium-size pan. Allow to simmer for about 25 minutes until done and the water has been completely absorbed.

2 Set aside 1/2 cup milk, stir the remaining milk with the cream and sugar into the rice and bring to a boil.

3 Cut the vanilla pod open lengthwise and scrape out the seeds with a sharp knife. Stir the cornstarch into the 1/2 cup of milk until smooth, then gradually add it to the boiling rice mixture, stirring constantly. Add the vanilla seeds and a pinch of salt, then allow the rice mixture to simmer for 15 minutes, stirring frequently.

4 Fill small dessert bowls with the rice pudding and allow to cool, then leave in the fridge for 3 hours. Dust with cinnamon to serve.

Tip

For variation, chop 1 3/4 - 2 1/2 ounces of plain or dark chocolate coarsely and add it to the cold rice mixture just before serving.

Melon Yogurt Drink
with Fresh Mint

Ingredients

¹/₄ Cantaloupe or honeydew
melon (about 10 ounces fruit)

1-2 tablespoons lime juice

2 tablespoons honey

1 ¹/₄ cups plain yogurt

³/₄ cup carbonated mineral water

¹/₄ bunch fresh mint leaves

Preparation
SERVES 4

1 Cut open the melon, remove the seeds and peel. Cut into quarters. Take one quarter and cut into small pieces. Blend together with the lime juice, honey, yogurt and mineral water in a food processor or with an immersion mixer until very fine and smooth.

2 Wash the mint and shake dry, then pluck the leaves from the stems and chop finely.

3 Mix the mint into the melon yogurt drink and fill the drink into glasses. Garnish with stems of mint (optional) and serve with ice cubes.

Lime Lemonade
with Vanilla Syrup

Ingredients

²/₃ cup lime juice

3 tablespoons grated lime rind

1 vanilla pod

³/₄ cup sugar

1 lime

ice cubes

Preparation

SERVES 4

1 Put the lime juice and the lime rind into a bowl, cover with 1 ¹/₄ cups water and allow to stand overnight.

2 Cut the vanilla pod open lengthwise and put into a pan with the sugar. Add 1 ¹/₄ cups water, bring to a boil and simmer for 10 minutes. Remove the vanilla pod and allow the vanilla syrup to cool for a while.

3 Pour the lime juice through a sieve into a bowl. Add the vanilla syrup, stir well, fill into a bottle and leave in the fridge.

4 To serve, wash the lime with hot water, rub dry and cut into thin slices. Arrange ice cubes and lime slices in the glasses, then pour in the cooled fruit juice.

Oriental Chai
with Cardamom

*For those who want that something special: This sophisticated
spiced tea is a welcome change to tea bags and filtered coffee*

Ingredients

1-2 teaspoons black tea
leaves

1 cinnamon stick

8 green cardamom pods

5 cloves

2 cups milk

4 tablespoons honey

Preparation
SERVES 4

1 Bring 2 cups water to a boil. Add the tea leaves, bring to
a boil and remove from the heat. Allow the tea to brew for
3-5 minutes, then pour through a sieve.

2 Roast the cinnamon stick, the cardamom pods and cloves
in a pan without oil, stirring constantly, until their aroma
becomes intense. Bring the tea and the herbs to a boil in
a pan and simmer gently for about 5 minutes.

3 Add the milk and honey, bring to a boil again, then remove
the pan from the heat. Allow the Chai to steep for 3-4 minutes, pour through a sieve and fill into glasses. Serve with
1 cinnamon stick (optional).

Tip

Use black tea varieties like Assam, Ceylon or Java
for your Chai. These are strong and full in flavor
and go very well with milk and honey.

Almond Milk
with Orange-Blossom Water

This is what hospitality tastes like: This refreshing milk mix is often served as a traditional welcoming drink

Ingredients

4 ounces almonds

$^2/_3$ cups sugar

3 cups milk

$^1/_2$ cinnamon stick

$^1/_4$ cup orange-blossom water

ice cubes

cinnamon powder, to dust

Preparation

SERVES 4

1. Put the almonds into a pot of boiling water and allow to swell for about 4 minutes. Pour into a sieve, drain, and allow to cool slightly. Remove the peel from the almonds with your fingers.

2. Put the almonds into a tall mixing bowl with $^1/_3$ cup sugar and blend very finely with an immersion blender. Put the almond mixture into a small bowl and cover with 1 $^1/_4$ cups water. Cover with plastic wrap and store in a cool place, preferably overnight.

3. The next day heat the milk in a saucepan. Add the remaining sugar and the cinnamon stick and bring to a boil. Remove the pan from the heat and allow the milk to cool. Skim the skin from the top of the milk with a spoon if necessary. Remove the stick of cinnamon again and stir in the orange-blossom water.

4. Pour the almond mixture into a sieve and allow to drain, reserving the almond water. Press out the remaining juice from the mixture using a spoon. Discard the solids. Stir the almond juice into the milk. Cover the milk mixture with plastic wrap and leave in the fridge for 2 hours. Serve the almond milk in glasses with ice cubes, and dust with cinnamon.

Index of recipes

Copyright

Photo Credits

Cover photos: Susie Eising (front cover); StockFood/Jean Cazals (back cover top and bottom); StockFood/Susie Eising (back cover center)

Jo Kirchherr (Styling Oliver Brachat): 8, 9, 51, 57, 63, 72–73, 79, 103–104, 105, 113, 127; StockFood/Damir Begovic: 35; StockFood/Michael Boyny: 29, 60, 71, 87, 115, 123; StockFood/Caspar Carlott: 67; StockFood/Jean Cazals: 19, 23, 37, 41, 48–49, 65, 75, 80, 85, 107; StockFood/Achim Deimling-Ostrinsky: 15, 17, 27; StockFood/Drool LTD, William Lingwood: 119; StockFood/FoodPhotography Eising: 4–5, 25, 59, 61, 89, 95; StockFood/Susie Eising: 1, 21, 28, 31, 33, 38, 39, 42, 43, 81, 83, 93, 96, 99, 100, 101, 116, 117, 125;

StockFood/S. & P. Eising: 6, 7 top left, 7 middle, 7 right, 47, 92; StockFood/Luzia Ellert: 34, 122; StockFood/Alena Hbrková: 53, 91; StockFood/Johansen: 97; StockFood/Joerg Lehmann: 86; StockFood/Barbara Lutterbeck: 22; StockFood/Renato Marcialis: 18, 77; StockFood/Kai Mewes: 7 (2nd from bottom left), 10–11, 45; StockFoodKarl Newedel: 7 (2nd from top left); StockFood/Kia Nu: 111; StockFood/Antje Plewinsky: 55, 69, 121; StockFood/Peter Sapper: 2–3; StockFood/Jim Scherer Photography: 54; StockFood/Amos Schliack: 109; StockFood/Maximilian Stock LTD: 7 bottom left; StockFood/ Martina Urban: 13; StockFood/Elisabeth Watt: 66, 108

Lamb Ragout (front cover): see recipe p.84